MW00945101

Chipper's Friends

The heartwarming story of
an imperfect dog

Written
By
Michelle Jansick

Lulu Publishing
Copyright © by Michelle Jansick 2013

Chipper's Friends
ISBN: 978-1-300-82578-4

by Lulu, Inc.
www.Lulu.com

This book is dedicated to children and animals who are waiting to be rescued. May these pages somehow serve as a way to bring them safety, hope, and love.

Note from Chipper

The stories in this book are based on my real life journey to find people who needed a friend like me. I made some minor modifications for narrative purposes, and changed the names of my friends in order to protect their identities. Some of the characters in this book are combinations of more than one person, but they are based on real people whom I am honored to call my friends.

*"I have found that when you are deeply troubled,
there are things you get from
the silent devoted companionship of a dog
that you can get from no other source."*
—Doris Day

Introduction

Normally I am not fond of taking a bath—but that morning was different—so instead of slinking out the doggy door to hide in the garage, I bravely stepped into the tub on my own free will. That day I was going to meet some new friends, and I wanted to look and smell my best.

I was excited and a little bit nervous at the same time. I wasn't quite sure what I would do once I got to the teenage homeless shelter, but I figured I didn't really have to have a plan. I just needed to make myself available, and the rest would take care of itself.

Some tough-looking boys were playing basketball outside when I arrived. Their hats were on sideways, so I wasn't sure I was cool enough to be their friend. But just then one of them saw me and shouted, "Look! There's a doggy!" He hurried over to pet me and asked if I knew any tricks. I showed him how I could Sit, Shake, and give a High Five. (I didn't Roll Over because back then I didn't know what to do with my butt.) He was so impressed that he asked me to play basketball with him. I politely declined, even though I was flattered, because I'm only twenty inches tall and lack opposable thumbs. I decided to go inside the shelter to see if I could find more friends.

On Sundays the kids have to do chores, so a girl was cleaning the windows and a boy was mopping the floors. A teenager wearing a white hooded sweatshirt introduced himself and told me all about the huge spider he used to have for a pet. He had bought it without asking his mom's permission, even though he knew she hated bugs. He grinned and said, "One day she found my spider in her bathroom—so she screamed really loud!" I wanted to ask if that was why he was living in a homeless shelter, but I sensed it would be inappropriate. Besides, I understood why he liked spiders. They are delicious.

A tall boy with the most wonderful smile I have ever seen walked up to me. He said I was a Good Girl, and I couldn't help but gaze into his kind eyes. He was wearing a Green Bay Packer sweatshirt, but I decided to love him anyway. I could tell he loved me too because he disappeared for a moment and came back with a paper cup full of water just for me. He said I reminded him of a dog he once had.

Just then, a man in a purple cap introduced himself to me. His long black hair was in braids, and I had never seen that before so I initiated the Emergency Barking System. No one seemed impressed. Mom told him I brought little Christmas gifts, so he agreed to gather the teenagers so I could give one to each of them. But instead he announced that I was there to search for drugs! I growled at him so they would know he wasn't telling the truth, and everybody laughed.

Passing out those little presents was a lot of fun because I got to meet all of the kids, and they were very nice to me. Twenty boys and twenty girls lived at the shelter. Some of them had been there for quite a while; others had just arrived. I wanted to know their stories. Why didn't they live in a cozy home with a Christmas tree and a nice yard for digging? Didn't they have anybody to love them? Why didn't their parents come looking for them?

After the kids thanked me for their gifts, they headed to the lunchroom. I waited around for a little while longer, and that's when a girl with baggy clothing walked up to me quietly. She slowly knelt down and started to pet me. I looked into her sad eyes and then kissed her hands until she smiled. She was the one who needed me that day. I knew what it was like to be a homeless youth because I had been one too.

1

Doggy Jail and Destiny

I grew up as a stray puppy on the streets of New Mexico. I was hungry, cold, and afraid. Some people captured me and took me to a shelter. Those were sad times because I didn't belong to anyone. Nobody loved me.

One day a Nice Lady bailed me out of doggy jail when I was eight months old. She loaded me into her van and then drove around picking up more puppies who needed saving. Several shelters had called her that week saying they would have to euthanize a total of 32 puppies if she didn't come for them. So she took all of us pups to her house, and gave us food and water. She had a lot of nice friends, and they put collars on each of us. Every collar had a number, and my number was 751 because I was the 751st puppy they had rescued that year.

All of us pups got to stay in cozy foster homes for a little while, and then we took car rides to a pet store that was hosting an adoption event for shelter animals. Nobody wanted me because I was so terrified of people that I peed whenever anyone got close. To this day, I am still embarrassed about that. I went to two adoption events, and all of the puppies got adopted except me. I started to lose hope.

It turned out that I had nothing to worry about because destiny popped me to my new mom on her 38th birthday. She fell in love with my bashful brown eyes, and it didn't matter to her that I lost control of my bladder when I was frightened. She knew I just needed a little confidence and a lot of love.

She took me home that night and carried me to my new back yard because I didn't know how to walk on a leash. We sat quietly beside each other under the stars, and then she gently put her forehead against mine. At that moment, I knew she would love me for my whole life. I didn't have to be afraid anymore.

My dad never had a dog when he was a kid, so I was his very first one and that made me extra special. He taught me how to do all sorts of fun tricks, and I tried my best to make him proud.

My mom needed a four-legged friend to take on daily walks, so I tried to be brave when she put the scary leash on me. At first I just stood there with my tail between my quivering legs and refused to move. Then I mustered up some courage and zigzagged forward, backwards, left, and right. I got tangled up and tripped her a few times as we walked down the street. Dad watched from the driveway and chuckled. Mom was very patient with me, and gave me treats for motivation. Eventually I got the hang of it, and we went exploring almost every day so I wouldn't get bored and she wouldn't get fat.

I don't know if you've ever heard the song Zip-A-Dee-Doo-Dah, but that's how it was back then. We covered miles and miles on dirt trails and sidewalks. We saw birds, prairie dogs, squirrels, and rabbits. We passed trees, rivers, mountains, and lakes. Neither of us wore a watch, and we traipsed around for as long as we felt like it.

My parents adopted me right after Thanksgiving, so I arrived just in time to celebrate their tradition of chopping down a Christmas tree in the Rocky Mountains. My dad was especially excited that morning. He gathered some tools from the garage and loaded them into the truck. Mom collected some mittens, coats, and stocking caps. I took myself outside to go Potty, and then away we went!

Dad accidentally went through a stoplight because he was thinking too hard about donuts. Mom giggled and agreed to take a delicious detour before continuing on our adventure. It was a beautiful drive, and I gazed out the window the whole way so I wouldn't miss a thing. Nothing could spoil that day for me, not even when Dad belted out the wrong lyrics to a Kenny Rogers song: "You picked a fine time to leave me, Lucille, with four *hundred* children."

We hiked all over the place in search of the perfect tree. Fresh snow covered the ground, and that was very exciting. I had so much fun that I kept forgetting why we were there, but Dad stayed focused and eventually he found exactly what he was looking for. Mom wanted our picture with the beautiful pine, so Dad and I huddled close together and I put my paw on his knee.

Mom and I watched Dad chop the tree down, drag it around for a while, and then tie it to the top of our truck. I was so exhausted from watching him work so hard that I slept the whole way home.

2

Sissies and Shopping

The next morning I sat beside my parents' bed and exhaled as loudly as possible until I got their attention. (Some dogs wake their parents by jumping on the bed or barking, but not me. I'm very respectful.) I was ready to do something exciting with my new family.

After breakfast, we loaded ourselves into the car and headed to the pet store for some quality education. Nowadays when you adopt a pup, you're supposed to take him to socialization classes so he can get into a good college later. It's important for us to learn important things like how to sniff another dog's butt. I absolutely loved my first socialization class. I played with little puppies and big puppies, young puppies and older puppies. We tackled each other and ran around the room as fast as our legs would carry us. The excitement was more than I could handle, and I threw up three times. The lady in charge had to throw away one of the toys because of me. She was nice about it, but I think she was glad when I left.

After our trip to the pet store, my parents took me for a walk. I was having a great time until my feet started to hurt because the sidewalk was so cold. I stopped and held up my paw so Mom would know I didn't want to walk any farther, but we were still several blocks from our house. She felt terrible and called the veterinarian for advice as soon as we got home. He suggested that my parents buy some dog booties so I wouldn't get frostbite when we went for walks on cold days. That's how I ended up owning a pair of bright red dog booties against my will. At first I decided to wear them cheerfully in exchange for free room and board—but then my dog cousin, Pepper, made fun of me so I kicked them right off. Pepper lives in the mountains and thinks booties are for sissies. He's probably right.

Mom decided to start taking me for walks inside stores on cold days because both of us enjoy having warm feet. It takes courage to walk around in stores. At first I was a little bit scared, but eventually I got used to all sorts of new sights, sounds, and smells. I even got to ride in elevators. Mom taught me to walk Close to her, and to Wait at the end of each aisle instead of rushing ahead. I didn't realize it back then, but she was starting to train me to be a therapy dog.

Employees gave me treats and called me a Good Girl. (It's great to be a dog because when you meet someone for the first time, they usually give you a treat. It's not like that with just any animal. People don't go around handing out treats to cats, birds, hamsters, or fish.)

Customers often stopped to pet me, and I always showed them exactly where I preferred to be petted—by putting my face on the floor and sticking my butt up in the air as high as it could go. It was my signature move, and it always made them laugh. Mom couldn't believe how quickly I had transformed from being a fearful, incontinent dog into one who absolutely loved people.

Mom took me everywhere dogs were allowed: home improvement stores, camping stores, pet stores, home furnishing stores, ranch supply stores, etc. I got to be kind of a big deal, and pretty soon I was making regular visits to a car dealership because everybody there liked me a lot. Sometimes Mom took me to the bank drive-thru, and that was very interesting. She would park the truck next to a machine, stick some money in a tube, and it would get sucked up into the sky. A few minutes later, the tube would drop back down with a receipt and a dog treat inside. It was amazing.

One day we were walking around a sporting goods store, and she took me over to a big see-thru box with water in it. She thought I would like to stare at some fish, but I was more interested in the people who were sitting nearby. They weren't like anybody I had ever seen before, and I was very happy when one of them asked if she could pet me. Even though I was still a puppy, I sensed that I needed to be very gentle with her. She asked a bunch of questions about me and said I was pretty. She giggled like a little girl when I shook her hand. Pretty soon, others in her group came over and started petting me too. They were innocent like children, but in grown-up bodies. They were special, and I loved them immediately. My mom was very proud of me and she smiled a lot because, as it turned out, she had big plans for me. I just didn't know it yet.

3

Flying Hamsters and Young Love

The nice thing about living in Colorado is that you get 300 days of sunshine, so Mom and I get to go on walks outside most of the time—even during winter. During those early days together, we usually walked in silence because we were so busy smiling. But one day she decided to tell me a story from her past so I could get to know her better.

She started with the day she came home from the neighbor's house with mice crammed into the pockets of her skintight jeans. She was six years old, and that was the beginning of her love of animals, or "aminals" as she called them back then. She had a lot of pets while growing up, even though she was allergic to most of them: a canary named Jingle Bells, a guinea pig named Sir Dinky, a frog named Kermit, a turtle named Scooter, six dogs, four hamsters, three rabbits, and one cat.

Mom tried to live without an animal when she went off to college, but she couldn't do it. She met a woman selling baby German Shepherds in the grocery store parking lot, but thankfully my grandpa was there to talk her out of doing anything foolish. It wouldn't be easy to hide a 75-pound dog in a tiny dorm room, and her roommate (whom she had not met yet) might not like the idea.

Mom compromised and got a hamster instead, even though it was against school rules. Sometimes he escaped from his cage and scurried down the hallway, but Mom could always find him by following the trail of screaming girls. When it was time to go home for Spring Break, she smuggled him through airport security in her coat pocket.

That was way before they paid TSA agents to pat down your private parts. Back in those days, you could skip through the airport carrying a huge bottle of shampoo (whereas now you can only carry several small bottles of shampoo). There was no reason to be scared to the level Orange, and you could burst into the cockpit midflight just to say hi to the pilots. But you were not allowed to hide rodents in your clothes. That was strictly forbidden. It's a good thing my mom was so sneaky. That little hamster got to fly all the way from Arizona to California, and no one was the wiser.

My mom was a senior when she saw my dad for the first time at an ice cream party in college. She thought he was so handsome that she immediately reserved a church for their wedding, but he didn't notice her because she was so short. They met for the second time at a bonfire, and by then she had chosen the color of her bridesmaid dresses even though he was busy admiring her taller girlfriends. Dad was a freshman, so meeting a bunch of new female friends all at once was thrilling.

When my dad asked his new group of friends if anyone wanted to join him for breakfast, Mom was the only one who said yes. When she didn't order anything to eat, Dad realized the only reason she came along was to be with him. She gazed across the table into his big blue eyes, and they were twitterpated over each other from that point on. Mom said she loved him, and that was a very big deal because she had never said that to any other boy. Dad told his friends back home in Minnesota that he had found his future wife, which was good since she had already mailed out wedding invitations.

During college breaks, they wrote letters to each other every day. People didn't have cell phones back then, so my parents recorded mushy messages to each other on a cassette tape and mailed it back and forth between California and Minnesota. That way they could hear each other's voice all the time without having an expensive long distance phone bill. Dad got a job and saved up some money for an engagement ring. He was very excited when he finally had enough cash to walk into a fancy jewelry store and buy the smallest diamond they had.

It was snot-freezing cold when Mom flew to the Midwest to see Dad during Winter Break. He drove her to Lake Superior and made her get out of the truck against her will. The wind-chill brought the temperature way below zero, and her toes turned green. They walked around in the pretty snow until they came to a bench, and that's when my dad knelt down to propose. Mom quickly said yes so she could return to the warm truck as soon as possible. She loved her engagement ring (because it was from my dad) and showed it to everyone who had eyeballs.

She wore her hair French braided on their wedding day because Dad thinks she's prettiest that way. He wore Martin the Martian socks, and they lit their unity candle with a butane torch. When the preacher said it was time for The Kiss, my dad snapped his fingers and all of the groomsmen marched into position while he grabbed a Mickey Mouse step stool for my mom to stand on (because she is so short). The guys formed a semicircle facing the giggling audience so my parents could have some privacy while they smooched.

Mom and Dad had their first fight as a married couple as they left the church parking lot. They argued about whether or not to take the freeway to the reception, and that would be the first of many future arguments about driving.

I could have listened to my mom talk all day, but our walk had come to an end and we were back home. She agreed to start telling me something about her past on our daily walks until I knew everything about her. She had 38 years worth of stories to tell me about, and I was excited to hear every one.

4

Reindeer and Virtual Bowling

I was due for some more practice in becoming a great therapy dog, so Mom decided it would be a good idea for me to make some new friends at a nursing home. It was cold and windy when we arrived, so I was anxious to get inside where it was warm. I had received a special invitation to visit the residents with Old Timer's Disease (or something that sounded like that).

I had been preparing for that day for quite a while. A few weeks earlier, my grandma flew in from California to visit me so I could practice being gentle with a very old person (she's in her sixties). To my knowledge, she doesn't have Old Timer's Disease, but she does have a hard time remembering that I'm a girl.

I passed the senior citizen test with Grandma, even though I licked all of her vitamins. I didn't jump on her, scratch her, or chew on her shoes. I did trample her while she was face down in the back yard, but that was only because Mom tied antlers to my head and made me star in her video called "Grandma Got Run Over By A Reindeer." Obviously I wouldn't be allowed to do that at the convalescent home.

When I walked inside the building, I saw a pretty lady with dark skin wearing a bright blue sweater. She was walking slowly down the hallway, holding onto the railing. She didn't say anything, but she seemed very happy because she had a big smile on her face.

Along came a man who had a walker with a teddy bear in the basket. He looked at me and said, "I love dogs." He petted me for a few seconds and then repeated two more times, "I love dogs." My mom had been worried that I would be afraid of walkers and wheelchairs, but I wasn't. In fact, I loved the walkers because they had tennis balls stuck to the legs. I would have liked to play fetch with the walkers, but no one else seemed to think that was a great idea.

Two ladies in wheelchairs were playing a board game, so we stopped to say hello. One of them was wearing fantastic red socks. She told us all about a pet poodle she had when she was younger—it lived 17 years! She asked if we had seen the movie *Hachi*, which is a true story about a dog in Japan who loved a college professor named Richard Gere. At that point I stopped listening, but not because I don't like Japan or Richard Gere. I had just spotted some popcorn on the table next to her and it smelled so delicious that I couldn't focus on anything else.

A birthday party was going on down the hall. Two people—one man and one woman—were wearing birthday hats. Everyone was very happy to see me even though I interrupted their bingo game. I performed my tricks for them, so they cheered and said I was very smart and a Good Girl. They all took turns petting me while I tried to eat a piece of chocolate on the floor. Everyone said I was pretty and had soft fur, which is true.

A very nice nurse named Suzie introduced herself and said, "You have to come with me to meet Gracie because she loves dogs!" On the way to her room, I met a nice man from Vietnam who kept calling my name and asking me for High Fives. I wanted to spend more time with him, but he was pretty busy watching a karate movie.

We found an elderly woman standing in the hallway, but it wasn't Gracie. Suzie the Nurse asked if she wanted to pet a cute doggy, but she shouted, "No!" I probably would have gotten my feelings hurt if I were a person, but I'm a dog so I cheerfully continued my search for Gracie.

She wasn't in her room. We found her alone in the lounge, crying. It's a good thing I was there because I knew exactly what to do. I put my paw on her knee so she wouldn't be sad anymore. It worked. She buried her face in mine and showered me with kisses. She asked me to give her nine High Fives, which I did. She wanted to impress me with her video game bowling skills, so I stepped aside for a moment to give her space. She knocked down all of the pins on her second try. Grinning from ear to ear, she was quite proud of herself and rightly so. I rewarded her with six more High Fives and three Shakes.

With that situation under control, I followed Suzie the Nurse to meet somebody whose name sounded like Miss Muffet. We found her lying quietly on her bed in a room with the lights off. Her fingernails were painted red, and she was wearing pink fuzzy slippers. She smiled when she saw me and asked, "What is your name?" Mom told her my name was Chipper, and she said, "What a nice name." A few seconds went by, and Miss Muffet asked again, "What is the doggy's name?" So we told her my name was Chipper, and she said it was a very nice name.

It started to snow outside, so it was time for us to leave. We had a long drive home, and Mom panics whenever there is a drop of moisture on the road. Suzie the Nurse took us to one last room where a man was sitting alone, watching TV in his wheelchair. She asked him, "Would you like to pet a cute doggy?" He smiled and nodded his head, so I showed him my tricks. He couldn't speak, but his eyes twinkled when he petted me. I sniffed his wonderful new white tennis shoes, and he chuckled with delight. He liked me so much that he tried to feed me his chocolate chip cookies. We only stayed with him for a few minutes, but as we stepped back into the hall, Suzie said, "That's the most I've seen him smile since he's been here."

On our way out of the nursing home, I noticed that the same pretty lady wearing a bright blue sweater was still walking down the hall, holding onto the railing. She was still smiling.

5

Rubber Bands and Granolas

Before I came along, Mom didn't have a consistent plan for keeping fit. It wasn't unusual for several days to go by before she remembered to exercise with her TV friends. Her lack of discipline was not without consequences. Sometimes she spent the last ten minutes of the routine lying on the couch trying not to vomit. One time she accidentally punched herself in the face.

I consider myself her personal fitness trainer. I motivate her every morning to go on a walk simply by pestering her until she gives in. One day when we were walking on a dirt trail near our house, she decided to tell me a story about when she and my dad were newlyweds in Arizona.

After the wedding, my parents moved to Prescott, and if you've ever been there, then you know it's very important to pronounce it correctly. The town's motto is "Prescott, like biscuit." If you say it wrong, some good ol' boys will drag you into the bushes and beat you with sticks.

Their tiny one-bedroom apartment was upstairs, and Mom immediately decorated it with dried flower arrangements. Dad said it was like walking through a dead forest. They didn't have air conditioning, and that summer was one of the hottest on record. (It didn't help that Mom ran into the wall and unknowingly turned on the heater for two days.) It was a miserable few months, and they probably would have died if not for being newlyweds in love.

My parents carpooled to work together in their little red truck. Dad worked at a camping store, where he helped women with hairy armpits (AKA "granolas") try on hiking boots. Mom worked at a shop down the street, where she was paid to sit on the floor and sell carpet. She had a kind boss who once cheered her up by giving her money to go buy a cheeseburger. One day when she was required to attend an early morning staff meeting, she gently protested by showing up in a robe and slippers. He rolled his eyes and smiled.

Later she worked at a lighting store, where she had another wonderful boss. Miss Karen provided an endless supply of smiles, hugs, and cinnamon rolls. Even if it only snowed one inch, she would call my mom and tell her to stay home and be safe. Mom worked there for five years and somehow got the reputation of being a great employee even though she accidentally shot a customer with a rubber band.

A co-worker invited my parents to go to a country dance with a group called Ruffles and Rawhide. Mom was ecstatic because swing dancing is one of her most favorite things to do even though she lacks rhythm and physical coordination. My folks learned how to swing dance in college, and they already owned cowboy boots because it's required by Arizona state law. Most of the couples in the Ruffles and Rawhide group had danced together for many years. A lot of them had matching outfits, and Mom loved to watch them move together with ease while the music played.

When Dad saw how happy my mom was at the dance, he agreed to take her to a Country Waltz class on Monday nights during football season. Yes, you read that right. During. Football. Season. If that's not love, then I don't know what is. That was when Mom started the tradition of giving out a Best Husband Award.

6

Harmonicas and Getting Kicked

On Sundays I cuddle with my dad on the couch to watch football. He wears his Minnesota Vikings helmet, socks, and Adrian Peterson jersey because that helps our team win. He sucks Mountain Dew from a straw so he can keep his helmet on during all the offensive plays. I have my very own Vikings bandana, and I wear it proudly around my neck. We give each other High Fives whenever they score a touchdown. We do not like the Green Bay Packers.

One day the phone rang during a Vikings game, and it was my dad's brother Jayme. He wanted to come visit us, and my mom told me I'd like him a lot. She was right. Uncle Jayme lives in a group home for disabled adults in Minnesota. He works at a hotel and rides the city bus to work. He likes to go bowling, loves to play the harmonica, and knows a lot about furnaces.

Jayme is visually impaired, but that doesn't stop him from sending texts from his phone or riding his bike (into mailboxes). One time during an outdoor church service, he twirled up and down the aisle playing his harmonica while everyone was singing. Jayme isn't like anybody else, and that's the best part about him. Mom likes his sense of humor, and he likes "the smile in her voice." One time they spent a whole hour giggling and clapping their hands to turn a lamp on and off.

A few days before Jayme came to visit me, Mom recorded his favorite shows on TV: *Judge Judy* and *Little House on the Prairie.* When he arrived, he plopped himself on the couch and listened to music on his headphones. I sat beside him, and he smiled and petted me. We spent hours like that, and I thought it was the best thing ever.

Later we went on a walk together, and Jayme held onto my leash. He grinned the whole time, and I did too. When we got home from the walk, we snuggled on the couch again and watched my very favorite movie, *A Dog Named Christmas.* It's about a boy like Jayme who springs into action after he hears an animal shelter employee ask radio listeners to provide a temporary home for a pup over the holidays. The boy begs his parents to let him foster a dog for Christmas, and before you know it, he convinces enough friends and neighbors to do the same until not one single animal was left at the shelter. Most people can't watch the movie without crying a little bit.

I rested my chin on Uncle Jayme's lap for most of the movie. I sat up to watch my favorite part when they showed all of the dogs in the shelter. Then I lay my head back down on Jayme's lap and he petted me. I think he missed most of the movie because he was too busy smiling down at me.

My mom decided that since I was such a Good Girl with Uncle Jayme, I was ready to continue practicing to become a therapy dog by visiting a group home for disabled young adults.

It was a winter day, and I enjoyed the car ride. I saw a herd of cows, a couple of horses, and a bunch of prairie dogs. Mom parked in front of the group home, and I noticed a dog park across the street. There were little dogs, medium dogs, and big dogs. I wanted to play with them and sniff their butts, but I didn't have time for that right then. I added it to my To Do list and saved it for another day. I had something more important to do. People needed me, and I sure as heck wasn't going to let them down.

Mom rang the doorbell, and a very nice man named Darin invited us in from the cold. I left a trail of snowy, wet paw prints on the floor, but Darin told me not to feel bad about it. I felt very welcome.

Just inside the entryway on the left was a girl named Chrissy who was eating cookies and listening to music on headphones. She was sitting in a rocking chair that glided back and forth. A blue blanket was draped over her legs and she was wearing an orange blouse. Her hair was in a ponytail, and she was one of the prettiest girls I had ever seen. When she saw me, she smiled so big that her eyes got squished up and I could hardly see them twinkling. She was very nice to me, and she told me all about her family's cocker spaniels.

A very friendly girl named Susan rolled her wheelchair into the room. She was wearing a green blouse and fuzzy brown slippers. She told me all about her family's collies and then asked me to Shake, so I did. She held my leash for a while, and she must have wanted to keep me because she held on tight when it was time for me to leave the room to go meet some more friends.

Darin told me I was a Good Girl and said he had thought about trying to get his Labrador Retriever certified as a therapy dog, but he was worried that her big, wagging tail might hurt somebody. I have a long tail and I wag it all the time, but nobody ever gets hurt. Darin took my mom and me to meet the staff. They were all volunteers, and they were working very hard in the kitchen to prepare special meals for the residents. I didn't think they would have time to say hello because they were so busy, but they all stopped and smiled at me.

Mom and I followed Darin into another room where five residents were gathered in a circle to greet me. One girl was wearing striped socks and pink pants that matched the color of my leash. They called her Hippie Holly because her shirt said "Peace" and "Love." She was in a wheelchair too, and there was a red pillow under her feet. She couldn't talk, but I'm pretty sure she was happy I was there.

Next I met a man named Robert who was wearing a black cowboy hat pulled down so far I couldn't see his eyes. He wanted to pet me, so I huddled close against his wheelchair for him to reach. I didn't realize Robert was blind until after I performed a few tricks for him, so that was a little embarrassing.

Just then a guy named Ernie kicked me, but it wasn't very hard because he was in a wheelchair. One of the nurses said he likes to kick everybody because he is "ornery." I had never been kicked before and it caught me off guard, but it was no big deal. It was good practice for me because if I ever volunteered at a children's hospital, I would have to let them do things like that (within reason, of course).

I guess Susan was already missing me from the other room because she rolled into our room with her wheelchair. She asked to hold my leash again, and we sat there smiling at each other for a while. Then it was time to leave so everybody could eat lunch. I had a great time and was happy to make so many new friends. If this was what therapy dogs did, then I was going to love it!

7

Timothy Hay and Crazy Kacey

I wanted to go on a walk the next day, but Mom preferred to stay inside and drink hot cocoa instead. She turned on some Christmas music and we cuddled together on the couch, gazing up at our tree and admiring the pretty lights. She looked at each ornament one by one, and some of them made her smile. I listened quietly as she told me a story about the Reindeer Ornament.

Grandma had given her the ornament about 14 years earlier: a little ceramic reindeer who cheerfully held a sign that read "Jeff and Michelle." As fate would have it, one day when that reindeer was just hanging on the tree minding its own business, Mom's pet bunny took notice and decided it looked quite delicious. He tugged it off the tree and onto the floor. Then he nibbled the edges off the reindeer's sign until it just said "hell." Mom always hangs the reindeer ornament front and center on the tree because she giggles every time she sees it.

Back when my mom was working at the lighting store in Prescott (like "biscuit"), a lady pulled up in the parking lot. She had a litter of baby bunnies and—within 15 seconds—Mom was cradling the newest member of her family. It was a very impulsive and irresponsible thing to do. She hadn't asked my dad first, nor had she gotten permission from the landlord.

Thankfully, it all worked out and Dad loved the little fuzz ball. They decided to name her *Wee* because she was so tiny. Wee lived with them for two months before they noticed that she was, in fact, a male.

Wee was a very smart rabbit, and he provided a lot of entertainment. He learned how to use a litter box right away. He waited beside the refrigerator whenever he wanted a grape. He made a buzzing sound whenever he was excited, and he loved to grab hold of the toilet paper roll with his teeth and then pull it all the way down the hallway.

Wee didn't stay tiny for very long; he grew up to be about nine pounds. A friend said he should have been named *Wow*. He could jump amazingly high. One evening when Mom and Dad were watching television, Wee darted around the living room and then vaulted himself over the back of the couch.

The only bad thing he ever did (besides ruining the reindeer ornament) was chew 36 buttons off the VCR remote control. He was very sweet and easygoing. When Mom decided to add a hamster to the family, Wee handled it in stride whenever Petie ran into him full speed during his wild hamster ball rides.

Petie, who turned out to be a female, added a lot of laughter to their days. One day she managed to stuff her cheeks with a paper towel that was still attached to the roll. Dad gave Petie a little piece of an old T-shirt, and she covered herself with it every morning like a blanket.

Petie got sick while Mom was at work one day, so Dad earned the Best Husband Award by taking the little fur ball to the vet. Poor little Petie squeaked when they used a thermometer that was too big for her little hamster bottom. Sadly there was nothing the doctor could do to save Petie, and she went to hamster heaven. Mom cried for a little while and Dad conducted a moment of silence.

A few weeks later—while Mom was at home burning a grilled cheese sandwich—Dad burst through the door excitedly. He had just seen a cage full of baby birds at a pet store. One of them climbed up a little ladder and squawked, "Pick me! Pick me!" Dad convinced Mom that it was time to add another member to the family, so they grabbed their piggy bank and found the little gray cockatiel anxiously waiting for them. They named him Bart because the yellow feathers atop his head reminded them of Bart Simpson.

Bart chewed 11 buttons off the TV remote control. He loved Dad but hated everything else: balloons, yo-yos, picnic baskets, Christmas, and Mom. Bart loved to spend hours peering down the dark crack between the couch and the wall. Nobody knew what he was hoping to find down there, but it was entertaining just the same. Sometimes Dad would wedge his head behind the couch to help Bart find what he was looking for, and Mom would laugh until she snorted.

Mom's beloved bunny, Wee, passed away one day because he got a big hairball stuck in his belly. She decided she could never endure the pain of losing another rabbit, so day after day went by and the apartment seemed terribly empty. Eventually Mom realized she could not live without a lop-eared friend. So she read books about bunnies and learned how to recognize when they were sick. She highlighted the important parts that talked about feeding them timothy hay to prevent hairballs. (Timothy Hay is not a person, it's a type of grass.)

My mom drove out to a farm and peered into a cage full of baby Holland lops. She chose the beautiful little brown one hiding in the back. She named her Kacey and smiled the whole way home. Perhaps this precious new friend would fill the void left by her beloved Wee bunny. Mom imagined all of the good times they would have together, skipping through sunny meadows while butterflies danced through the blue sky.

Kacey turned out to be the Rabbit from Hell, inhabited by Satan himself. She was a real jerk compared to Wee—solid proof that no two kids turn out alike (one can be a real loser) despite having the same loving parents. In hindsight, Mom learned that it's better to choose a pet based on personality rather than looks, especially if it is glaring at you from the back of the cage, plotting your death.

Even though Kacey was only eight weeks old, any layperson could see that she had a bipolar disorder. One minute she'd sigh with contentment while my mom was petting her. The next minute she would lunge at Mom, growling with nasty big pointy teeth. (If you don't think rabbits can growl, just ask my grandma.)

Mom resisted the urge to smother Kacey with a pillow, and instead got her spayed in hopes that she would mellow out (and because female bunnies have a 90% chance of getting ovarian cancer if they aren't spayed). She took the vile creature to a vet who was knowledgeable about rabbits. Mom tried to hide her disappointment from the doctor when Kacey survived the operation with no anesthesia complications.

The day after surgery, Kacey chewed up a doorframe and bit Mom five times, thus shooting the "Spaying Creates Gentler Pets" theory all to hell. Sure, rabbits are prey animals and it's normal for them to bite when they feel threatened (which is why, contrary to popular opinion, they are not good pets for young children). But that's not why Kacey bit people. She simply enjoyed it. She used to sharpen her teeth on the edge of the bathtub, and I'm not making that up.

My parents considered auditioning her for the TV show "When Animals Attack," and then using her earnings for euthanasia. But eventually they learned to accept the bad hand that life had dealt them. Mom memorized the Serenity Prayer and joined a support group for battered women.

8

Cops and Cheeseheads

My mom likes to lollygag on walks. Sometimes she will stop and sit down beside a lake for five whole minutes just because she thinks it's pretty. I don't have time for that sort of thing, so I whimper to let her know I prefer to keep moving. I have places to go, things to do, and squirrels to chase. She usually ignores my whimpers and makes things worse by taking pictures of everything imaginable. She worries that if she doesn't capture life's "moments" with the camera, then she will forget them.

I can't relate because my memory is superb. If you were to hand me a map of our neighborhood, I could show you every single place I have seen a squirrel in the past two years. Sometimes I walk down the sidewalk on my hind legs so I can get the best possible angle for spotting squirrels in trees. That's what I was doing one day when Mom decided to tell me more about life before Chipper.

After five years of living in Arizona, my Dad got a new job in Wisconsin. Mom decided to go there with him so she could watch his detached earlobes whip around in the wind when the car windows were down. They loaded up all of their belongings, including a silly bird and crazy rabbit. They waved goodbye to Arizona in the rear view mirror, thus marking an end to the first chapter in their life as a married couple.

Right away, my parents noticed that people in Wisconsin do strange things. They put noodles in their chili and say "stop-n-go light" instead of stoplight. They say "beg" when they mean "bag," and "a boat" when they mean "about." They don't put fences around their yards, and they spend a lot of money on Halloween decorations. You can't find any good Mexican food there, and state law requires you to eat fish on Friday nights even if you aren't Catholic.

Wisconsin folks eat a lot of cheese, so they are usually in need of a laxative. (If you see one of them wearing a cheese-shaped hat, that means they are constipated.) Wisconsinites love their Green Bay Packer football team more than life itself. They dress newborn babies in green and yellow jerseys even though they would rather cheer for the Minnesota Vikings. They love to sit outside on cold metal benches in subzero temperatures to cheer on their team. The waiting list to buy season tickets is so long that you have to wait for someone to die before you can have their seat.

Wisconsin smells pretty bad, on account of all the cows and paper mills. A lot of folks work the night shift in factories, hoping somebody will retire so they can work the day shift. Most of the people who live there have never even been to the Mall of America, even though it's a major tourist attraction just a short drive away. People visit there from all over the world because it has three Taco Bells inside of one building.

Wisconsin was the first place Mom had ever seen the seasons change because she grew up in San Diego where the weather is perfect every day (and therefore boring). The snowfalls were beautiful, and there were always plenty of snowplows to keep the roads safe. She loved to smell the lilac bushes in the springtime and go camping in the summer. She was overwhelmed whenever the spectacular fall leaves changed from yellow to orange to red. In Wisconsin, you can't just hike around in the woods whenever you want to because someone will shoot you. You have to wear a bright orange vest so they know you aren't a deer. Dad tried to take Mom hiking without a vest during hunting season but she didn't fall for it.

My mom really loved living in Wisconsin, except for the day she was almost arrested for stealing her own car. She was just driving to the grocery store, minding her own business, when a policeman stopped and asked for her license and registration. She hadn't been speeding (she drives like an old lady), but when the cop checked her license plate number, it was reported stolen. She sat patiently in the car—looking at the flashing red and blue lights, thinking about prison life—while he made some phone calls. He sized Mom up and figured she wasn't a car thief, so he didn't hold her at gunpoint or make her wear handcuffs. All of her paperwork checked out just fine, so he let her go.

Mom had never heard a tornado siren before she lived in the Midwest. The alarms went off all the time, and she took every one of them very seriously. While other apartment tenants were outside grilling hamburgers, Mom would frantically gather the pets, shove her treasured photo albums into a backpack, and bunker down in the community laundry room to await imminent death.

Mom didn't die during that tornado season, but her eyesight did start to deteriorate so she had to—yep, you guessed it—buy a bigger television. She got a job at an electronics store so she could buy one at cost, and Dad never loved her more than he did at that moment. They loaded the 57" box of fun onto their little truck, and then pushed it up the stairs into their tiny apartment. "Larger than Life Larry" was the best thing they had ever owned, and they couldn't stop smiling—until a piece of timothy hay got stuck in the vacuum a few days later.

As Mom was trying to unclog the hose using a long wire hanger, she heard a scraping sound and knew right away what she had done. To her horror, she found a long scratch on the front of the brand new television. Mom waited nervously for Dad to come home and then reluctantly confessed what she had done. He quietly went to the bedroom to get control of his emotions. Then he emerged a few minutes later, hugged her and said, "I still love you, but from now on there are going to be some new rules."

That was right around the time Mom got a hankering to learn how to play a new musical instrument. She didn't have enough money to buy an actual guitar, but that was just a minor obstacle. She cut out a piece of cardboard and drew lines to resemble strings and frets. She found websites that showed her where to place her fingers for certain chords, and she practiced for hours.

A friend thought she was an idiot until he handed her his guitar and she played a flawless D chord. My dad learned to play the guitar too, but he didn't have to use a piece of cardboard. His redneck friend Chip gave him one, on the condition that he didn't play any Neil Diamond songs. Eventually my mom's grandpa gave her his guitar, which significantly increased her credibility in the musical community. (Not too long after that, my parents formed their own band. I'll tell you more about that later.)

9

Zombies and Peeing on Pee

My mom's life motto is *You Never Need A Reason To Panic*. Like many women, she has the ability to anticipate everything that can possibly go wrong in any given situation. So even though there is a humongous off leash dog park across the street from our house, I wasn't allowed to go there until I was about a year old. Mom worried that I would run away and not be able to find my way back home. She feared that I would be attacked by a coyote, a rattlesnake, a mean dog, or a zombie. Thankfully, she finally came to the conclusion that it was worth taking those risks in order for me to reach my full happiness potential.

Even though the dog park is just a few footsteps from our house, Mom decided we should drive there so I could practice Car Etiquette. I'm not allowed to jump out of the car as soon as she opens the door. I have to Sit and Wait until I am calm and focused so I will be obedient when I get inside the park. This requires a lot of self-control, which not all dogs have. One time I heard a dog approaching from a mile away. His head was sticking out of the car window, and he was shouting at the top of his lungs, "I'M ON MY WAY TO THE DOG PARK! I'M COMING! I'M ALMOST THERE! YIPPEEEEEEEE!!!!!!"

Mom made it a point to read all of the caution signs at the entrance. She memorized what to do if we saw a coyote: be loud, look big, throw rocks. And she knew how to avoid rattlesnakes: don't lift up rocks, don't peek in bushes, don't poke them with a stick. Eventually she stopped worrying and started smiling. We made it a habit to go there almost every day.

I really can't even describe to you how amazing the dog park is, but I'll try. It is 410 acres of pure bliss. The trails are endless, and I love the feel of the soft dirt under my paws. There's a pond next to a big shade tree, and that's the best place to hang out in the summer. The lake freezes over in the winter, but then I get to play in the snow and that's even more fun.

I haven't even mentioned the smells yet, and that's the very best part! I can press my nose to the ground and discover something about every dog who has ever been there before me. I can smell urine on a tree and tell you how tall that dog was just by the height of the pee mark. I heard somebody say once that a dog's sense of smell is one hundred times greater than that of a human. I don't know for sure if that's true, but it must be because my mom never presses her nose to the ground when we're at the dog park. I bet she would if she could smell everything that I can.

On a normal day I can hold my bladder for several hours, but when I'm at the dog park I make it a point to pee every thirty seconds. I pee in the dirt, on rocks, and near bushes. Sometimes I even pee on another dog's pee. It's fantastic. You probably think that's stupid, or maybe even disgusting—but if you were a dog you would understand.

I love being around all of the people and their dogs. Sometimes I am so anxious to meet somebody that I forget about my own personal safety and run right up to them even if they are speeding along on a mountain bike.

I have learned two very important things at the dog park: (1) grasshoppers are delicious, and (2) I can run much faster than most dogs. Sometimes I am able to coax ten dogs into chasing me at the same time! Mom shakes her head and laughs when she sees me running in giant circles at warp speed, followed by an entourage of Chihuahuas, Great Danes, and everything in between.

Playing with Great Danes is an extreme sport. They are my favorite breed because they are always very friendly and playful. But they are so big that they scare me a little, and I get an adrenaline rush from it like people do when they jump out of airplanes. I shriek in fear when I play with Great Danes, but then I always go back for more.

I have several friends at the dog park that I play with almost every day. Ernie and Bert are a couple of German Shorthaired Pointers who were rescued from a shelter after they failed to become good hunting dogs. Then there's Brownie, and I'm pretty sure he is a terrier of some sort. His grandma takes him there all the time. He is a little bit taller than me, and his fur is brown and curly. We love to go on long walks together in the sunshine. Sometimes we go swimming in the lake with other dogs. (Actually I don't swim because that's kind of scary; I prefer to walk around in the shallow parts.) The only bad thing about going in the lake is that I have to take a bath when I get home because I smell bad and I'm covered with mud.

Mom says the best thing about taking me to the dog park is that I take a nap for the whole rest of the day. I am much better behaved when somebody takes me out on a daily adventure. Sure, I have a nice back yard to play in, but that gets boring. I love to wander around, explore new places, and hang out with my doggy friends.

10

Cactus Attack and Fowl Play

Mom decided to take me for a walk on Big Dry Creek Trail one day. It's a dirt trail that winds around a neighborhood, a pond, and two schools. I was having a great time until I accidentally pooped on a small cactus. Part of the cactus got stuck in my leg. I managed to get it off using my teeth, but then to my horror, the cactus got stuck to my tongue! I had a panic attack, as I'm sure you can imagine. I thought I might die. But finally I pulled myself together, took a deep breath and spit it out. It was very traumatic. Mom and I walked together in silence for a while after that, and then she decided to tell me another story about Wisconsin to cheer me up.

The crazy rabbit's behavior did not improve after she moved to Wisconsin. Kacey jumped behind the TV and chewed through the electrical cords of everything my parents owned. She tore up carpet and ruined baseboards, even though Mom kept her supplied with an endless amount of chew toys like baskets and cardboard boxes. She bit anyone who reached into her cage to fill the food dish or change the litter box. Dad worried that she would try to kill them in their sleep. They tried to find an anger management class for rabbits but came up empty handed. Finally they had an epiphany, which is a fancy word for "a great idea."

Bunnies bond in pairs, so Mom and Dad decided to get a friend for Kacey. Off they went to search for a new little bunny companion who could transform the demonic beast into a gentler soul. (FYI it's a terrible idea to bond two males because they will try to kill each other.)

Shane was a little, charcoal gray bunny with soft, shiny fur. She was lop-eared like Kacey, but one of her ears stuck up in the air because it hadn't drooped yet. Shane was not only beautiful but had a very sweet, friendly personality too.

Kacey and Shane became best friends right away. They were inseparable. They groomed each other, played together, and rested close against each other. Mom let them out of their cages whenever she was home because rabbits need to run and play just like any other animal (except, of course, a worm). Kacey had a more positive attitude toward life, and the world became a better place for almost everyone.

Life wasn't easy for Bart, especially when he got his wings clipped. One day he fell off the shower rod, ricocheted off the toilet, and plummeted into Kacey's litter box. Dad felt sorry for him because it is humiliating to fall into someone else's poop.

Bart lost most of his tail feathers after a traumatic incident with my dad's shoe. Then one of his head feathers got caught (and yanked out) in Mom's new glasses. Shortly after that, his ankle bracelet got stuck above his knee. At one point, poor Bart felt so discouraged that he tried to kill himself by pecking at an electrical outlet.

The bird struggled with "object permanence" issues, meaning that he could not grasp the concept that Mom still existed after she left the room. Bart had developed a fear of flying by then, so he felt it was too risky to follow her around the apartment. Even though he still didn't like her, he chirped incessantly when they were apart. Every chirp was the same pitch and volume, in a steady annoying rhythm that made Mom want to flush him down the toilet.

Bart passed away unexpectedly at the age of six, and Mom assured everyone that no fowl play was involved. He just woke up one morning and didn't feel very good. Later that day, he went peacefully up to the Big Birdcage in the Sky.

11

Butterfly Wings and Nail Polish

I was very flattered when my mom's friend, Rachel, invited me to join her for the Muscular Dystrophy Walk at the local mall. Rachel was in charge of pediatric hospice, and her team was called the Butterfly Kids. They wanted to win the contests for Biggest Team and Most Team Spirit, so they needed my help. I agreed immediately, and we started preparing for the big day.

Some of the boys made colorful posters to hold up at the mall. Mom helped me make my very own little blue poster that said, "Go Butterfly Kids!" Rachel gave me some stickers shaped like doggy paw prints to put on it.

Some of the girls glued colorful glitter to plastic clackers so our team could make a lot of noise at the mall. The clackers scared me, so Mom brought one home to help me get used to the sound before the day of the walk. She shook the clacker while I ate breakfast, and I got used to it in no time.

The kids decorated some cardboard butterfly wings to attach to the back of their wheelchairs. They had a lot of fun doing that, and I hoped it made them forget about being sick for a little while. Rachel gave everybody matching blue T-shirts with a picture of a butterfly on them. She gave me my very own blue T-shirt so I could be like everybody else on the Butterfly Team. It was very nice of her to do that, and it made me feel special.

Unfortunately it also made me feel like I was wearing a straight jacket. I was too uncomfortable to walk, sit, or lie down in it. Mom saw the sad look in my eyes and decided not to make me wear it. So I thought I was off the hook until she came up with Plan B.

Plan B turned out to be a terrible idea. Mom thought it would be fun to surprise the kids by having me wear some butterfly wings to the mall walk. Since it wasn't Halloween, she couldn't find any to buy at the store so she decided to make some herself. She looked on the Internet and found instructions for making wings out of two metal hangers and a pair of nylons. There was a tiny hole in the nylons, and that led to an interesting chain of events.

Mom used some pink nail polish to keep the hole from getting bigger, and it looked so pretty that she decided to use the entire bottle to decorate the wings. Later that night when we were asleep, Mom woke up feeling like she was going to throw up and pass out. She curled up and went to sleep on the bathroom floor for a few minutes and then the carbon monoxide detector made a loud, terrible noise.

It was only nine degrees outside, so it wasn't easy for us to leave the house right away. Mom quickly bundled up in her coat, stocking cap, gloves, and warm boots. Then she took me out to the driveway and we had a slumber party in the warm car while she called the energy company. Dad wasn't home that night, so he missed out on all the fun.

We only had to wait one hour for the repair man to arrive, and I helped Mom pass the time by going out for two potty breaks in the frigid cold. Long story short, the fumes from the nail polish made my mom sick and triggered a false alarm on the carbon monoxide detector. She felt pretty dumb but was glad to be alive just the same. Dad still likes to tease her about that night. He tells her that she almost became a Darwin Award (a form of natural selection in which someone removes herself from the gene pool in a stupid manner, thus improving the quality of the surviving generation).

Mom decided not to make me wear those toxic butterfly wings because, even though they were beautiful, they were too big and kept sliding sideways. She borrowed a pair of bright pink butterfly wings from our five-year-old neighbor instead. Those wings fit me much better, and my dad said I looked very pretty in them.

My mom is not what you'd call a "morning person." She's not really a "night person" either. Dad says she only has one good hour from noon to 1:00 PM. I try not to judge her since I myself require 13 hours of sleep, plus a late morning nap.

It was 8:00 AM when we arrived at the mall. Inside was a band playing really loud rock music, but I wasn't afraid. There were kids, wheelchairs, and service dogs everywhere. It was very exciting, but I managed to stay calm and focused on everything my mom asked me to do.

While we were waiting for The Walk to begin, people pointed and smiled at my pretty pink butterfly wings. One of them asked Mom if they could pet me, and she said yes because I wasn't a service dog on duty. I was a therapy dog (in training) who was there to have fun. News traveled fast, and a whole swarm of people rushed over to love on me. Little kids ran up and threw their arms around my neck. I thought I had died and gone to heaven. I wagged my tail just as fast as it could go.

Everybody said I was very cute and sweet, which of course I was. They wanted to know my breed, and Mom told them I was a shelter mutt (which is the best kind). Just when I thought things couldn't possibly get any better, someone spilled some delicious popcorn on floor. I was only able to sneak a quick nibble before Mom told me to Leave It.

I got to meet a mascot from the fire department. He was dressed as a Dalmatian wearing a red fireman hat. He was very tall, and he reached way down to pet me on the head. Most dogs are probably afraid of mascots, but I wasn't. I liked him a lot.

A bloodhound with the Search and Rescue team introduced himself to me, and I wondered if he had ever helped a missing child find her parents. I saw a man carrying a 4-month-old black Lab puppy who was training to be a service dog. Everybody thought she was adorable even though she wasn't wearing any butterfly wings.

We only made one lap around the mall because it's hard for people with muscular dystrophy to go farther than that. I could have run full speed around the mall 25 times without stopping, but I had plenty of fun walking slowly with my team.

Steven, a Butterfly kid, made loud noises with his clacker—but I wasn't afraid because I had listened to it all week at home. The wings on the back of his wheelchair were painted yellow with the words "FIND A CURE" written in purple crayon. His family held up a bright green sign that said "GO STEVEN!" My favorite thing about him was the wonderful dimple in his chubby little cheek.

Rodney's butterfly wings were blue, with colorful plastic jewels glued to them. Disease had stolen the use of Rodney's hands and feet, but not his smile. Mom gently pushed a dog treat into his disfigured hands, and he laughed when I took it from him. Rodney was really nice to me, and I loved him a lot.

Children with muscular dystrophy can get sick easily, so many of them stay inside all winter long just to be safe. Some of the Butterfly kids couldn't come to the mall walk because they had a cold. We still won the contest for Biggest Team, but we didn't win the prize for Most Team Spirit because we were up against a team of enthusiastic cheerleaders with bright red pom-poms.

After the lap around the mall, Rachel gave me a big hug and thanked me for coming. I had the best time ever, but it was time for me to leave. I was very thirsty and had to pee.

12

Sweet Tea and Happy Dancing

Colorado is known for having a lot of lean people in great physical shape (my mom can do 12 push-ups on her knees). Triathletes train here from all over the world because the high altitude makes their workouts challenging. It is not uncommon to see people riding their bikes along the side of the road, and most of them are decked out in fancy bright uniforms as if they are in a very serious race.

One day my mom and I were out on a walk having a great time, when all of a sudden we heard somebody yell in a very loud voice, "ON YOUR LEFT!" We panicked, got ourselves tangled in the leash, and peed a little. A bicyclist was fast approaching us from behind, and we barely got out of the way before he sped past us at 500 miles per hour. After a ten-minute humor delay, we laughed at our silly selves. We made a pact that in the future we would remain calm and casually move to the side of the path whenever a maniac shouted at us. With a good plan of action in place, we relaxed and Mom decided to tell me another story.

After about five years of living in Wisconsin (the state ranked #1 in beer consumption), my parents moved to Memphis, Tennessee (the city ranked #1 in violent crime). When they learned that it was cheaper to buy a house than rent one, Mom excitedly printed off twenty houses she had found on the Internet. The realtor looked at the addresses one by one and refused to take her to see any of them because they were in "unsafe neighborhoods." He drove my folks past a mall where thieves hid under cars to slash the heels of shoppers as they loaded purchases into their trunks.

Mom was afraid to leave the house for four years. She finally got her first cell phone so she could call 911 if someone stabbed her on the way to the library. She doesn't care for new technology, but Dad loves to have the latest thing the moment it is available. He gently prods my mom into accepting new gadgets into her life. Without him, she would still be listening to eight-track tapes and watching movies on a Beta VCR.

Mom thought of herself as a "Memphis Belle" because she ate black-eyed peas, drank sweet tea, and used the phrase "fixin' to." Dad said she was more like a "Memphis Ding-a-ling." When people in Tennessee say the word "paper," it sounds like "piper." There's no such thing as fast food in Memphis because everything happens very slowly there (except for a vine called kudzu which grows a foot per day). No one is ever in a hurry, not even the squirrels. The heat and humidity are so bad in the summertime that you feel the need to shower every five minutes. You have to run your air conditioner all night because it is still a thousand degrees at midnight. Even if it did cool off in the evenings, you'd still have to keep your windows shut because of all the murderers running amuck.

My parents didn't like Memphis very much, but they loved their house. It was a nice little brick home with big trees and flowers of every color. It came with a fenced back yard that was perfect for rabbits who needed a place to happy dance. Mom planted a garden for Kacey and Shane so they could eat carrots and parsley to their hearts delight. Whenever the weather was nice, she would sit outside with them for hours, keeping an eye out for hawks and cats. According to the veterinarian, Kacey had gotten a bit too chubby in the Midwest. But after a few weeks of running and twirling through her back yard paradise, she slimmed down quite nicely to the tune of 4½ pounds.

Kacey and Shane got to have their very own room in that house, which is a little bit ridiculous. Mom painted the walls mauve and used stencils to make rabbit designs. Dad hung a shelf on the wall, and she filled it with stuffed animals. They installed wood laminate flooring, and then Mom sewed a blanket so the bunnies could rest on something soft. She loved to walk down the hallway and peek in to find the two friends snuggling side by side on that blanket, as close as they could possibly be. There's a saying that people who have animals live longer, and I'm pretty sure it's true.

If ever there was a bunny built tough enough to survive life in Memphis, it was Kacey. She tackled the world fearlessly. She chased down a cat in the back yard and pounced on a pair of lightning bugs while they were trying to mate. She attacked a roll of paper towels and outsmarted a homicidal hawk. She designated her little gangster self as Head of Security in the rabbit room and conducted herself with such vigilance that my parents didn't see her sleep for two years.

While Kacey remained on high alert 24/7, Shane slept so soundly that sometimes Mom had to poke her to make sure she wasn't dead. Lacking the street smarts of her sister, she engaged in such activities as eating a fly swatter, getting her head stuck in a drinking cup, and throwing herself into the trash can twice. She ate two doorstops and chewed through Dad's favorite set of Christmas lights. She confused the neighbor's Super Grover kite for a hawk and hid under a bush, paralyzed with fear until Mom came to her rescue.

Word spread around Memphis that there was a grown woman who had a room just for her rabbits, so Mom became known as The Crazy Rabbit Lady. She wrote an article about bunnies so people could learn how to take good care of them. Kacey and Shane posed side by side in their room for a photograph, and they were featured in the local newspaper. (That wouldn't be the last time a member of my family was featured in the Memphis paper, but I'll stop there for now. I'm getting ahead of myself.)

13

Beta Fish and Yellow Ribbons

My mom was born with a fear of airports. She's not afraid to fly; she's afraid she won't be able to find the plane before it takes off without her. She was on her way to the airport to catch a flight to Alaska when she heard on the radio that a plane had crashed into the side of a tall building in a place called New York. She parked her car in the lot and went inside. Crowds of people were gathered around a TV to watch the news. A few minutes later, a second plane crashed into another tall building. Everyone was very frightened and confused. All of the flights were cancelled, and life wasn't the same after that.

Some bad men decided that they hated our country, so they killed thousands of innocent people. Everybody cried that day, and they were afraid in a way they had never been before. Once the initial shock wore off, they decided to be courageous instead of hiding in fear. They put American flags up in their yards and went to football games to cheer on their favorite teams. The President put some people in charge of making sure nobody ever attacked our country like that again. And he prepared for war.

A lot of brave men and women hugged their families goodbye and headed off to fight the war in Iraq. My parents tied a yellow ribbon around the tree in the front yard because their friend,

Wade, was among that group of brave soldiers. They were very proud of him for serving our country. Wade's friends helped to take care of his family while he was gone. They mowed his lawn, assembled pink bicycles for his daughters, and threw a birthday party for his wife. They even helped to look after his *male* beta fish named Esther Sally Lucy.

Mom couldn't imagine being without my dad for a year, especially if she knew he was in danger every day. She was very, very thankful for the sacrifices made by Wade and his family to keep everyone in America safe. A woman in Tennessee decided that all of the soldiers needed to receive letters and treats from people back home, so Mom and her friends adopted a squad. They sent some letters, and the soldiers were very grateful to get them. It was the highlight of their day whenever the mail delivery person called out their name. Mom learned how to make brownies that could withstand the high desert temperatures, and one soldier said they were "out of this world." She was very relieved to hear that because the brownies she normally made at home always turned out soggy in the middle and rock hard around the edges.

Most of the soldiers wrote back and said how much they missed their families and couldn't wait to come home. Being in Iraq was frightening, and they didn't like seeing their friends get hurt. Three of them were injured by bombs, and one was awarded a purple heart.

When Wade and his fellow soldiers finally got to come home after a year had passed, there was a big celebration. Mom helped blow up 500 balloons and make a bunch of Welcome Home posters. Over 1000 people came to the homecoming party, including a senator and reporters from three TV stations. There were a lot of smiles, tears, and hugs.

After the party, Mom went home and cut the yellow ribbon off of the tree in the front yard. It had faded from the sunlight because one year is a very, very long time.

14

Freckles, Tigger and Gus

We live within walking distance of a pretty little golf course with a dirt trail that weaves in and around it. It's one of our favorite places to walk, so we go there often. Mom likes it because of the beautiful mountain views, and I like it because it borders a prairie dog habitat. That's where we were when she decided to tell me more about life in Tennessee.

Mom worked part-time at a flower shop when she lived in Memphis. She wanted to volunteer at the local animal shelter on her days off, but she couldn't bring herself to go there because it was such a sad place to be. Then one night she saw a TV show about a mean man who hurt his little dog, and that was that. Mom cried and made a decision that she would have to toughen up because there were dogs at the pound who needed to be loved.

When she arrived at the shelter, she asked what she could do to help. A staff member named Michael said someone had left a box of puppies on the doorstep that morning. He needed help giving them medicine, and Mom was very happy to hold them still. People dropped off litters of puppies all the time. Some of them got adopted, but many of them were euthanized. (It wasn't the shelter's fault. Thousands of puppies are put to sleep every day because people don't spay and neuter their pets.)

After Mom helped Michael with the little puppies, she asked if there were any dogs that hadn't been on a walk for a while. As it turned out, a dog named Butch needed some exercise. He had been brought into the shelter with a collar embedded in his skin. It took a few moments for my mom to find the courage to approach Butch because she was afraid of big dogs, but eventually she put a leash on him and he was absolutely thrilled. As soon as they got outside, Butch joyfully flung himself across a small ditch and nearly dislocated my mom's shoulder. She made a mental note to take a smaller dog out next time.

That animal shelter was one of the best around, and it had a big fenced area for the dogs to play off leash. Butch stretched his long muscular legs by running and leaping across the yard. He was happy for the chance to play outside, and Mom hoped he would find somebody with a big yard to adopt him. After a little while, Mom took Butch back to his kennel and traded him for a medium sized terrier named Freckles.

Freckles had been brought to the shelter because "his fur doesn't match the furniture." He was white with brown spots, and he was extremely friendly and playful. He smiled a lot and wagged his tail back and forth. He was very good at playing fetch, and Mom thought he would fit perfectly into a family with kids.

Next it was time to play with a very sweet dog named Tigger. A man had abandoned him at the shelter because "he's too friendly." Apparently he wanted a guard dog instead. Tigger stole Mom's heart in five seconds. He was a little shy at first, but then he followed her around and let her rub his belly. He had mostly black fur, with little specks of white on his face and paws. Mom played with him for a while, and then it was time for another dog to have his turn in the sunshine.

Normally Mom is afraid of Rottweilers, but Maggie had a sad look in her eyes and it was easy to see why. Her ribs were showing, and it looked as though they had been that way for quite some time. Mom took her out to the big yard and sat quietly beside her under a tree. Mom asked Michael if she could give Maggie some food, and he nodded his head. She had been thrown out of a moving car right after she gave birth to a litter of puppies. Michael assured Mom that he would personally make sure to give her plenty of food so she could reach a healthy weight.

The last dog Mom walked that day was Blackie. He was an elderly dog with wiry black and gray fur. His owner had dropped him off at the shelter because he was "too old." Blackie didn't run and jump like the younger dogs did because of his arthritis, but Mom could tell he enjoyed having soft dirt under his paws instead of hard concrete.

Mom couldn't get to all of the dogs that day. There were too many of them and not enough volunteers, which made her very sad. On her way out, she saw a forlorn five-week old puppy peeking at her through metal bars. Michael was locking up the shelter and ready to go home when she asked if she could take the little pup home so he wouldn't have to spend the night alone in a scary place. Michael smiled and said that would be fine. A construction crew had found the pup on a job site. He was covered with fleas when he arrived at the shelter, and he almost died of anemia.

Mom smuggled the pup home while Dad was out of town. She and her tiny new friend cuddled together in front of the fireplace that evening. She kept him in a little cage beside her bed through the night. The next day they played together in the yard, running through the grass and bouncing in the fall leaves. She didn't want to say goodbye to the fuzzy fur ball, but Dad was due home the next day. So she found another volunteer to foster the little guy until he was old enough to be adopted. (Shelter employees don't have time to tend to young puppies, especially if they need to be bottle fed around the clock. They depend on volunteers for that.)

Mom went back to the shelter a few weeks later, and that time she took Dad with her. Maggie, the skinny Rottweiler, had reached a healthy weight and Mom didn't even recognize her. She bounced around the big yard with such a huge grin on her face that my parents couldn't help but laugh. Freckles wasn't there anymore because he had been adopted.

My folks played with a couple of beautiful Huskies that had been surrendered to the shelter when their owners got divorced. Two sweet Beagles named Harley and Hanna had been kicked out of their house after the arrival of a new baby. Then there was Gus, a little Lhasa Apso with an adorable underbite. His owner had passed away.

Mom went to get her favorite little dog, Tigger, but she found him curled up in a tight ball in the corner of his kennel. He was very sick, so she wrapped him in a blanket and held him in her lap. She wanted to take him home and snuggle in front of the fireplace, but it was too late to help him. She stayed until the shelter closed, then said goodbye and cried the whole way home. Tigger passed away that night, alone on a cold, cement floor with no one to love him.

A few months later, Mom learned that the shelter was planning to euthanize 40 dogs that week. Even though it was a "no kill" shelter, they were way over capacity and couldn't find enough volunteers to provide temporary foster homes for the dogs until they could be adopted. Mom was very sad, and so were the shelter employees. She took some dogs out to play in the big yard and wondered which ones of them would be gone the next time she went to volunteer.

She couldn't sleep that night. She worried what would happen to Butch, Maggie, and Blackie. Would someone come in time to save the adorable Beagles? Would anyone rescue the Huskies? And what about little Gus? Mom wanted to take all of them home with her, but she was worried they would harm her bunnies. So she cried and moped around until she heard that something wonderful had happened.

A reporter with the local news brought a camera crew into the shelter. People all over town heard about the predicament, and pretty soon they started pouring through the doors. Butch and Maggie got adopted. So did Harley and Hannah. The Huskies found a new home with a lot of land for them to run. Nobody wanted old Blackie, but some nice people picked him up and took him to a sanctuary where elderly dogs are given the chance to live out the rest of their lives in a kinder, softer place. By the end of that day, 43 dogs were adopted and not a single one had to be put to sleep.

15

Fake John Denver and Wasps

The nice thing about living in Colorado is that there is always something fun to do. A lot of folks have to save up a bunch of money for airplane tickets to visit, but we're just a hop, skip, and a jump from all sorts of beautiful mountain towns. We can wake up any old morning, pack some lunches, and be hiking in Breckenridge or Keystone by noon. We are very grateful for that privilege, and we make it a point not to take it for granted.

Mom found out about a John Denver Tribute concert in Estes Park, so she invited my grandma to fly out from California. They were very excited to hear Fake John Denver sing, but then my mom got the stomach flu the very same night Grandma arrived at the airport. That's how the Summer of Bad Luck got started.

Dad caught the flu from Mom, so she took me on a walk while he threw up at home. We went to Coal Creek, which is my favorite trail in the summertime because there are plenty of shade trees and a creek where I can cool off my paws. We were almost done with our hike when my mom stepped wrong and fell down in the dirt. She heard her ankle snap, and I didn't know what to do for her. She limped back to the truck in pain instead of calling my dad for help because he was at home with his head in the toilet.

By the time we got back to the house, Mom's ankle was purple and swollen. She had to wear a special boot for two weeks and then go to physical therapy for six weeks. I tried to comfort her but secretly I was depressed because she couldn't take me on walks for a while. Dad got a head cold the day after he got over the stomach flu, so nobody was available to take me on an adventure for several days. It was terrible for me.

When Dad felt better, he took my mom on a date while I stayed home and got 15 wasp stings on my face. Mom gave me some Benadryl, and Dad sat beside my doggy bed until I felt better. My parents launched a war against those wasps the next day. Even though it was hot outside, Mom wore a long sleeve shirt, long pants, leather gloves, and a ski mask. Dad made fun of her outfit and was confident he would be safe wearing a T-shirt and shorts. He was wrong.

Mom soaked the nest with a can of wasp killer, and then dad knocked it down with his Super Soaker water gun. He thought he could run faster than the wasps could fly, and that's how he got stung on his arms and legs. Mom wanted to say "I told you so" but she didn't because it's not nice to kick somebody when they're down. Dad's arm got infected and turned bright red and swollen. He had to call in sick for work and take antibiotics until he felt better.

Since Mom couldn't take me on walks until her ankle healed, she played with me every day in the back yard instead. She was sitting down after a nice game of fetch and that's when it happened. She asked me to come sit next to her, and I don't know what went wrong, but somehow her hand collided with my tooth. It didn't break skin (because I wasn't trying to bite her), but it severed a nerve and she had to get an expensive surgery to fix it. The doctor warned Mom that she would have to wear a splint for a while, and she wouldn't be able to use her main hand for two whole weeks. She was slowly becoming a paraplegic.

Dad is really good at a lot of things, but he can't cook and he's a lousy nurse (even though he tries his best). They agreed that the best way to stay alive and avoid divorce was to ask Grandma to come help, so she did. Grandma cooked fantastic meals and cleaned the house better than anyone had ever cleaned any house in the history of the world. She drove my mom to the grocery store and helped her put on makeup so she wouldn't feel hideous. She tied plastic bags on Mom's arm so she could take a shower instead of smelling like a sewer. Best of all, she took me on walks and washed my toys. I wanted her to stay forever, but eventually she had to go back home.

My parents had planned to spend all summer taking me on long mountain hikes, but we had to change that plan on account of Mom's injuries. Instead we found some rugged mountain roads and Dad drove us through the forest in the 4 x 4 truck. We stopped every now and then to go on short, easy walks while Mom's ankle healed. Things were going great until she knelt down on a rock to take a picture, and that's when she got Fat Pad Syndrome. (I'm not making that up. It's a real thing.)

The nurse figured Mom probably hurt her knee skiing, so she was surprised to hear that it was actually a "photography injury." Mom grinned and said, "The picture turned out great!" and the nurse responded, "Good. Maybe you can sell it to pay for your medical bills." Over the next couple of weeks, Mom hyperextended her pinky finger, sprained her wrist, got a head cold, two canker sores, a chapped lip, and an ingrown armpit hair.

Mom was feeling discouraged one day, so she took herself to her favorite restaurant while Dad was at work. She decided to pamper herself by asking the waiter to forget the garden salad and bring her chocolate cake instead. He asked if she was serious and smiled when she said yes. She washed down the chocolate cake with some coconut shrimp bites that were so good that she couldn't eat them with her eyes open. The world seemed like a better place after that, but only for a very brief period of time (forty-five minutes).

Our bad luck continued when my face collided with Dad's knee in the stairwell, and I chipped my front tooth. It hurt so much that I couldn't eat for a couple of days, and I had to have surgery to get it removed. Mom was really worried about me going under anesthesia, but I was very brave and did just fine. (My dad is afraid of the dentist, and Mom has to bribe him with treats just to make him go.)

When the Summer of Bad Luck was finally over, my parents and I thought about everything that had gone wrong over the past few months. We agreed that things could have been much worse, and we were thankful to have each other.

16

Drunken Goats and Purple Drool

Mom couldn't take me on a walk for 46 whole entire days during the Summer of Bad Luck, so I'm sure you can imagine how happy the two of us were when we were finally able to get back to our daily routine. Mom giggled as she watched me walk because my ears bounced up and down and my tail wagged constantly. Everyone who saw me described me with the same word: happy. And I was! Mom and I spent those days walking side by side, smiling. It had been so long since she told me a story that I had almost forgotten about our tradition. I listened intently as she shared more memories of Tennessee.

There's not much to do in Memphis unless you like to drink beer with a goat or rummage through Elvis' old stuff, but my parents have a knack for making things less boring. They watched a possum use a crosswalk, saw a lazy road crew paint a yellow line over a dead skunk, and listened politely while a salesman tried to sell them their own car.

Mom learned that some cockroaches can fly, and you could hear her scream a mile away. She accidentally burned a hole in the bathroom floor and melted a cup on the stove. She served a sandwich to one of Dad's buddies without remembering to remove the wrapper from the salami. And she had surgery to remove skin cancer from her forehead (she considers the scar to be one of her best features).

Dad maimed himself with the weed whacker but told everyone he was scathed by bullets. He tried to kill a fly with a towel but ended up snapping himself in the eye. He shocked himself while changing a light bulb and was disappointed when he didn't develop superhero powers. He passed out Batman valentines to friends at work, and earned the Best Husband Award by saving a sparrow that was trapped in the neighbor's gutter pipe.

It's hard to stay in love when you live in Memphis because the sticky heat makes you hate everyone. But my parents tried their best and formed their very own mediocre band called Purple Drool. Dad got an electric guitar, and Mom played the drums using kitchen pots and pans. They knew exactly how loud they could play without disturbing the neighbors because Dad turned up the amp and sent Mom outside to listen from the curb.

The tornado sirens followed my parents from Wisconsin to Tennessee. Mom quickly became a pro at herding the family into a tiny, windowless bathroom in the center of the house. The bunnies—Kacey and Shane—sat with her in the dry bathtub while Dad (who was there against his will) sat on the toilet lid and played guitar.

They celebrated their ten-year anniversary by going on their first real vacation—meaning they rented a car and a hotel room instead of staying with friends or family. Dad waited till Mom fell asleep and then sneaked out to buy a dozen roses so she could see them on the dresser when she woke up on their special day.

A couple of months later, Dad celebrated his birthday by getting three gray nose hairs. Mom thinks it's a shame that most folks don't say how much they like you until your funeral. So she asked my dad's friends to finish the sentence, "What I like about Jeff is…" and then she put their 46 answers inside a box and wrapped it up. One friend wrote, "He's the most intense fun person I've ever known." Another said, "He is kind, trustworthy, loyal… and always willing to help a friend in need." Dad felt pretty special after reading what his friends thought about him.

A couple of weeks after Dad's birthday, one of the deadliest hurricanes in American history destroyed much of Louisiana and Mississippi. One good thing about living in Memphis was that my parents were just a car ride away from helping folks after Hurricane Katrina.

Dad spent some time clearing branches and trash from people's yards so there would be enough room for FEMA trailers. Debris was stacked 25 feet high on both sides of the streets. There were televisions, washing machines, record albums, picture frames, and toys lying in the dirt. Clothing, towels, and blankets were hanging from trees.

Mom saw a big tree on the shore with a hand-made wooden sign that read "God bless this tree." Under that were the names of three survivors who had clung to it during 125 mph winds and a 30-foot tidal wave that reached ten miles inland.

Three months after the storm, people were still living in tents all over the city. Other folks stayed in their houses even though they were infested with toxic black mold. They couldn't cook for themselves (most of their kitchens were ruined), nor did they have transportation or money to buy food at the store. Mom met a young man on a four wheeler who was having trouble delivering food to a homebound elderly couple because the storm had washed away all of the street signs. The Red Cross served three hot meals a day. (Mom ate one of those meals in the back of a garbage truck on Halloween while delivering candy to kids.)

Survivors needed somebody to listen to their story. Many of them had barely escaped death, and most of them lost friends or relatives. A petite woman named Marie pointed to a house across the street and said, "Fifty-seven of us hid in that attic during the storm. The water came up 18 feet high and I thought

I would die because I can't swim. I still can't sleep at night." Mom gave her a hug, a blanket, and a new pair of white sneakers.

A lady named Lynne sat in her front yard wearing a bathrobe. With tears in her eyes, she said, "The water came up to my nose and mouth. My neighbor drowned." Mom asked if she needed a hug, and then gave her a coat and some bed sheets.

My parents kept walking until they came across a soft-spoken elderly woman sitting on a bench, staring out at nothing. How many days had she spent sitting there with piles of rotten debris lining her street? She was emotionally paralyzed after losing her home and her brother during the storm. Mom gave her some warm pajamas, a pair of slippers, and a teddy bear. Then she walked away with a heavy heart, wishing there was something she could do to change the grandma's past and offer hope for the future.

When my parents returned to Memphis, Mom found an ad in the paper urging people across the country to adopt a family whose lives were devastated by Katrina. My folks signed up for the program and were soon matched up with a family who had two little boys. Mom sent them a pen, a self-addressed stamped envelope, and a questionnaire asking what they needed. They sent it back with a request for pillows, baby shampoo, and other basic necessities. Mom had gobs of fun shopping for them and bought everything on their wish list. She sent a disposable camera so the family could take pictures of themselves and return it so she could put faces with names. The box arrived on the youngest boy's birthday, and the mother cried when she opened it.

Mom decided to make another trip to Mississippi, this time to help hurricane victims sign up for the Adopt-a-Family program. She knocked on the door of an 83-year-old widow. A sweet little old woman wearing a bathrobe and a hospital bracelet introduced herself as Mrs. Harvey. She invited my mom inside right away and asked her to shut the door so she wouldn't feel a draft. She tearfully told Mom that her son died in the storm.

She relived that horrendous night, remembering the desperate sounds of neighbors begging her for help. She hadn't been able to reach them, and she was sure they had drowned. She was still living in her unsafe house because she couldn't access her FEMA trailer without a wheelchair ramp.

When Mom told folks like Mrs. Harvey about the Adopt-a-Family program, they were very touched and relieved to learn that somebody somewhere cared enough to help them in their time of need. Mom hurried home to ask friends and relatives to adopt the people she had signed up for the program. They agreed to help right away, but a lot more assistance was still needed so my mom wrote an article and sent it to the Memphis newspaper in hopes that they would publish it. She sent pictures and described the new friends she had met.

The newspaper published the article and photos in a two-page spread. Total strangers found Mom's number in the phone book, and help started pouring in. A middle-aged woman called to say the article had inspired her to make a road trip with supplies for the survivors. She asked for a list of needed items and an address for where to deliver them. "I have time and money and I want to help," she explained. The woman adopted a family that day and asked her friends and relatives to do the same.

Mom's friend, Amy, printed out the newspaper article and put it on the counter at work for customers to see. One man read it and stood there in silence for a long time. After he cleared the knot from his throat, he handed Amy a check for $200 and told her to give it to my mom to use however she felt it could best help the victims. Amy's dog ate the check that night, or most of it anyway. Mom couldn't stop giggling, but Amy was on a humor delay because she was the one who had to explain to the man what happened. Amy showed him a picture of her dog and what was left of the destroyed check. He chuckled and gave her another one.

A lot of people adopted hurricane families, but still hundreds more were on the waiting list. So my mom sent an e-mail to the local TV station and asked them to promote the Adopt-a-Family program. They said yes, on the condition that they could come take her picture and interview her about it. Mom was caught off guard when they sent a video crew instead of a photographer, and that's how she got the nickname Blinky. She was so nervous—and the light from the video camera was so bright—that her eyes were closed the whole time. Actually they weren't just closed; they were blinking and flittering as if she were having a Grand Mal seizure.

Mom was feeling rather embarrassed by the whole thing until she received a phone call from someone who had seen the news that day. "I'm Mrs. John Hope, and I'm 89 years old," she explained. "My husband and I want to help but we are too frail to travel to the Gulf Coast." The sweet elderly couple had several cans of corn and green beans to donate, but they weren't physically able take them to the post office. When Mom offered to pick up the items and deliver them to the hurricane survivors, Mrs. Hope was thrilled and said, "Oh, thank you! We want to help so badly and now we can."

17

Falling Up Stairs and Daisies

Stairs are a real challenge for me, which is a problem since I live in a tri-level house. At times I am emotionally paralyzed by memories of falling *up* the stairs and knocking the wind out of myself. It has happened more times than I can count because my parents took forever to figure out that I cannot properly launch myself without the aid of a non-skid rug. Sometimes I have to sit at the bottom of the stairwell and psych myself up for a few seconds before I find the courage to catapult myself through the air.

One day after a fairly traumatic stairwell incident (my rug was in the washing machine), Mom decided to comfort me by taking me on a walk and telling me another story from her past.

My parents knew it was time to move away from The South when they accidentally used the phrase "might could" while talking to friends. Dad was offered a job in Denver, and they jumped at the opportunity. Some friends threw my parents a farewell party and helped load the moving van on a day that was hotter than two cats fighting in a wool sock.

My folks sold their house in Memphis and bought a smaller house on a smaller lot for twice as much money in Colorado. It was worth it. The mountain views were spectacular, and they were ecstatic to live in a place where they could go camping without hearing gunshots through the night.

When they pulled the moving van into the driveway of their new home, a squirrel jumped out of the big pine tree in the front yard. He landed on the roof and then squeezed through a hole leading to the attic. Mom and Dad were tired from the long road trip, so they made a mental note to deal with the critter later. They unloaded the moving boxes and went to sleep.

At 6:00 AM on the dot, they heard a scratching sound above the master bedroom ceiling. The squirrel was done sleeping, and it made sure that everyone else was too. My parents went outside in their pajamas to watch when it exited the attic so they could block the hole. A few minutes turned into a few hours, and a few hours turned into a few days. Dad boarded up the hole, but the squirrel had more than one entrance.

Daily battles continued each morning, beginning promptly at 6:00 AM. It turned into a massive covert operation involving friends (also in pajamas) using walkie-talkies to conduct reconnaissance missions from the empty lot next door. Dad realized that the squirrel left the attic whenever it heard him leave for work, so he instructed Mom to sit in the truck (with hot chocolate) and wait for the signal to start the ignition. The critter didn't fall for it, and an hour later they decided to regroup and come up with a new plan.

Although Mom was gradually warming up to the idea of using a .22 rifle as a last resort, she convinced Dad to buy a live trap at the home improvement store. He put it in the attic and left a little trail of cereal. It worked. Sort of. The "Live" part of the "Live Trap" did not work. The little pest must have died of fright during the traumatic event. As much as Mom hated that squirrel, she cried that evening and couldn't eat her dinner.

Kacey and Shane loved Colorado, but Shane started to develop some health problems shortly after they arrived. When Mom went out of town to visit a friend, Dad noticed that Shane wasn't eating anything. He earned the Best Husband Award that year by staying up all night with her.

Shane passed away soon after that, and Kacey was so sad over the loss of her best bunny friend that she gave up biting and growling for three whole days. Everybody knew how much Mom loved Shane, so they did what they could to make it easier on her. Friends brought over some food, and the little boy she babysat showed up with a bouquet of bright colored daisies.

From that day on, Mom tried her best to keep Kacey from getting too lonely. Sometimes they had slumber parties in the rabbit room, and Kacey was grateful for the company. She loved to rest her little head on Mom's pillow, and Mom loved her little bunny kisses.

Kacey spent her days hopping through the grass—and sometimes snow—in her Colorado back yard. Her favorite spot was under the big lilac bush, which was a good hiding place from the hawks, eagles, and owls that flew overhead. Mom always kept a close eye on the little bunny to make sure she was safe. Only one bad thing ever happened to Kacey outside, but it was nothing serious. Mom accidentally closed the screen door without telling Kacey, so the poor bunny bounced off of it and landed on the patio with her paws aimed up at the sky.

Kacey was 11 years old by then, and she became very sweet and affectionate in her old age. She loved to snuggle on the couch every evening, stretching her feet way out to achieve maximum comfort. She snorted with contentment whenever Mom petted her fuzzy little head. Those were happy times for Kacey, except for when she fell off the couch while scratching an itch.

At 10:00 PM every night, Kacey stood on her hind legs in front of the TV to let Mom know it was time for a carrot. Then she followed Mom up the stairs to the refrigerator. At bedtime, she hopped to her room and went to sleep under her favorite cardboard box.

18

Frogs and Santa Claus

Mom hurried to the The Kissing Step when she heard Dad come home at the end of the day, but he was in no mood for a Welcome Home smooch. He burst through the door with a worried look on his face and told Mom there was an outbreak of emphysema going around. She giggled, and that was the day he learned the difference between the words "emphysema" and "influenza."

Sometimes when I least expect it, my dad stops on his way home from work to buy a new toy for me. One day he brought me a frog stuffed animal, and it was love at first sight. Froggy was green, and he held a pink heart with the words "Love you." For the next few days, I gently carried Froggy everywhere I went. I played with him in the family room, the bedroom, and the computer room. (I did not play with him in the kitchen because I am not allowed in there.) We watched television and took naps together on the couch. I took him upstairs and downstairs. I tried to take him outside when I went on potty breaks, but Mom wouldn't let me because Froggy was an "inside" toy. So I carried him to the door and left him there so he'd be the first one I saw when I came back inside.

I loved him and knew we would be friends forever... until I chewed his leg off. I still feel a little bit guilty about that. In my defense, I wasn't trying to hurt him. I just wanted to know what he looked like on the inside. I was worried Mom would throw my maimed friend away, but she smiled and gathered all of the white stuffing strewn across the floor. She got her sewing machine and repaired the green amputee while I sat beside her trying my best to be patient. As soon as Froggy was ship-shape (minus one leg), I smiled and gently lifted him off of her lap.

A few weeks later, Mom asked if I'd like to help her pick out a Christmas gift for a little girl named Emily. I agreed immediately and was very excited. Emily was from a kindergarten class in the poor section of Denver. Some of her classmates didn't have enough to eat. They didn't have coats, warm stocking caps, or mittens. Some of them lived in a homeless shelter, and others in an orphanage.

Grandma came to visit, and Mom took us to the store to buy presents for Emily. Grandma bought the little girl a pink coat and purple mittens. Mom bought her a princess dress with a matching tiara and jewelry. I didn't find anything to buy right away, mostly because I was having a fantastic time shopping and didn't want the day to end. Salespeople walked up and asked to pet me, and since we weren't in a big hurry, I impressed them with my tricks and gave them High Fives. That stuff just never gets old.

It wasn't easy trying to decide what to get for Emily, but then there it was: a pink frog. I was confident that Emily would love that pink frog as much as I loved my Froggy. Mom helped me get the stuffed animal into the cart, and I cheerfully trotted to the cash register, grinning from ear to ear. We paid the lady and she gave me a treat. Then we went home and wrapped all of the gifts in red and green paper. Mom wrote "With Love From Santa" on the tags so Emily wouldn't know everything was from us.

I didn't get to go to the school the day Mom and her friends delivered gifts to the kindergarten class, but Mom told me all about it so I felt like I was there. The teacher's name was Miss Sara, and she was the best teacher in the whole wide world. When some of the children couldn't afford to buy school uniforms, she used her own money even though she didn't have a lot of it. She had a very nice smile, and she smiled a lot. She loved every student in her class, and they loved her right back.

The kids were all sitting quietly on a colorful rug when Santa walked in and surprised them. I wish I could have seen the looks on their faces! They all took turns sitting on his lap, and he gave each of them a present. One boy got a toy truck. Another got an airplane. One girl got a new tea party set, and another got—of course—a pink frog.

Most of the children were talking, laughing, and showing each other their gifts. But one little girl sat quietly in the middle of the chaos, smiling as she looked at her new picture book. She whispered "Wow!" every time she flipped to a new page. Miss Sara asked the kids to sing some Christmas songs, and they did a great job. They knew all of the words, and Santa was very impressed.

19

Stranger Danger and Bob

One day Dad woke up and Mom was nowhere to be found. He walked through every room in the house and called her name but she didn't answer. A few minutes later, he heard the garage door open and in walked Mom dressed in a bathrobe. She explained that she had looked out the bedroom window and seen a Lhasa Apso wandering around by himself in the street. Worried that he might get run over, she followed him through the neighborhood. When she knelt down to coax him near, he yelped "Stranger Danger!" and ran home.

Mom tried to rescue lost dogs all the time (unless they seemed unfriendly, in which case she called animal control to help). She kept a leash and dog treats at home and in the car, even though she didn't own a dog. Dad thought it was ridiculous.

One day when she was on her way to see the allergy doctor, she spotted a large dog resting in the shade on the sidewalk. Even though Mom was a little bit afraid, she decided to see if the dog was friendly and she was. She coaxed her into the car and called the phone number on her ID tag. The owner was very happy to get Mom's call because the dog had just given birth to a litter of puppies, and they were getting very hungry.

A few months after that, Mom was driving home from the grocery store when she saw two big dogs walking through a neighborhood by themselves. One was a German Shepherd with a hip injury of some kind. He could only walk a few feet and then he sat down to rest. Mom worried that he had been hit by a car. She wanted to help, but she knew she wasn't strong enough to hoist him up into the truck. While she tried to decide what to do, she spotted two mail carriers. She asked for their assistance, and was delighted when they agreed. Both dogs were very sweet, friendly, and… heavy! Mom could never have gotten them into the car by herself, and she was very grateful for the help.

Luckily the dogs were wearing ID tags, so she knew their names were Oscar and Nutmeg. Like many dog tags, these were scratched so badly that she could barely read the phone number. She called and the receptionist at a veterinarian's office answered. The woman offered to keep the dogs until she was able to contact the owners, so Mom drove Oscar and Nutmeg there. The staff was very nice and they helped the German Shepherd out of the car. Mom was relieved when the staff said he hadn't been hit by a car. His medical records showed a history of arthritis, which had no doubt been aggravated by romping through town all day.

Dad hated it whenever Mom saw a lost dog, probably because he worried he'd have to keep it if she couldn't find the owner. But Mom never asked to keep the dogs because of The Agreement. They had decided long ago that they definitely didn't want a dog for a pet. Dogs were smelly, destructive, and needy. They were expensive and noisy. They weren't as soft as bunnies and they drooled on everything. There was no reason to discuss it. They absolutely, positively, without a doubt, did not want a dog. Until they met Bob.

Dad was outside cleaning the garage when a little Jack Russell Terrier came running by, clearly having the time of his life. Dad reluctantly went inside and told Mom because he loves her even though he doesn't always love the things she does. Sure enough, Mom got out the dog treats and the leash and called out to the bouncing blur of happiness. The little guy came running toward her at top speed with a big smile on his face, and she escorted him to the back yard.

He wasn't wearing any ID tags, and animal control was closed for the weekend. Dad decided to give the temporary houseguest a name. "Bob is a good name for a male dog," he said. "It's simple and you can spell it the same way forward and backwards."

Bob was very smart. He knew how to do tricks and was very obedient. My parents took him on a walk, and even though he was just a midget, he had the strength of Samson and Tarzan combined. They borrowed a doghouse from a neighbor, but Bob didn't want to sleep outside by himself in the cold. Mom didn't want to bring him into the house because she was worried he would attack little Kacey. So she put on a stocking cap and snuggled in a sleeping bag with Bob in the garage. He fell asleep right away, snug as a bug in a rug.

The next day, Mom took a picture of Bob and posted signs all over the neighborhood. Nobody called looking for him, and my parents couldn't believe it because he was such a good little pet. They probably would have kept him if they hadn't been so concerned about Kacey's safety (Jack Russell Terriers are known for their rabbit hunting skills). Sadly they called animal control to come pick him up. He was taken to a shelter, where he joined hundreds of other dogs waiting for someone to love them.

My parents did a lot of hiking that summer, and Dad decided it might be nice to take a dog along. He became obsessed. When he woke up in the mornings, he looked out the window hoping to see a puppy walking around by himself. Mom wanted to get a small dog, but Dad insisted on getting one that was too big for her to dress in silly outfits. He spent every evening gazing at shelter pups on Petfinder.com and wanted to adopt all of them. But Mom was still worried about Kacey's safety, so a dog would have to wait until her little elderly friend passed away.

In the meantime, to satisfy their need for a canine companion, they decided to foster puppies for a rescue group. Mom knew she'd be able to keep them in a pen at a safe distance from Kacey. Thursdays became Mom's favorite day of the week because that's when she got new foster puppies. She had fun setting up the puppy pen and spreading out the Winnie the Pooh blanket for her four-legged guests. It wasn't easy to choose which ones to bring home because they were all so cute. Sometimes she brought home the entire litter, and Dad rolled his eyes around and smiled. He loved it when Mom fostered puppies because that meant he could play video games without being nagged.

She got to foster a litter of fluffy white pups that had been on the television show *Animal Hoarders*, so they were pretty famous. She named them Mickey, Minnie, Tink, and Jiminy. They were a lot of fun and made cute little squeaky sounds. Then she fostered an adorable pup with a broken leg. Skip, as Dad called him, had a bright green cast and I guess that's why he got special privileges. Since he was a bit groggy from pain meds, Skip got to snuggle against my dad on the couch during Video Game Night.

After that, Mom fostered a pup named Sarah who was afraid of everything and everybody. It was very sad. Mom had to keep her on a leash during potty breaks because otherwise she would dart fearfully around the yard. Mom patiently gained her trust by sitting quietly on the couch for hours holding the terrified pup. Instead of giving Sarah a bath on the first night of her arrival, Mom filled the dry tub with blankets and pillows. The two of them snuggled in there for a long time so that Sarah would learn that the bathtub was a safe place.

Mom decided that Sarah needed another foster puppy to teach her how to be happy and carefree, so Zoey came to visit for a while too. At first Sarah hid under the lilac bush for a long time watching Zoey play with toys. Then when Zoey finally fell asleep, Sarah creeped slowly out of the bush to retrieve one toy at a time while Mom watched from the corner of her eye and smiled. A few days later, Sarah improved so much that she WAGGED HER TAIL and even fetched tennis balls. Mom cried when she was adopted by a nice family who promised to give her the patience, confidence, and love that she deserved.

Before long my parents had fostered 55 puppies, and they resisted the urge to adopt … until they met me.

20

Slinkies and Screamy Houdini

My parents couldn't resist my sweet personality, and they knew right away that I would make a perfect addition to their family. But the final decision wasn't up to them; it was up to Kacey. Mom sat on the couch and held the bunny while Dad slowly led me toward her with a firm grip on my collar. I sniffed Kacey, and she wasn't afraid of me. I licked her forehead, and she pounced on my face with a growl. She showed me who was the boss, and my parents laughed. I loved Kacey, and she tolerated me. It was official. I had finally found a family to call my own.

I would never have done anything to harm my new lop-eared friend, but Mom and Dad made sure I never had the opportunity to fail. They set a lot of rules for me. I had to be very gentle with her because rabbits are wimps. I wasn't even allowed to bark at her because she could have a heart attack, and I'm not exaggerating.

Kacey's room was off limits, which was disappointing because she had a slinky that looked like a lot of fun. She also had a pillow made of corduroy that she liked to lick when she wasn't busy shredding cardboard boxes and running through the forts my parents made for her.

Kacey and I didn't get to play in the yard together because my parents knew she might hop around in a way that triggered my prey drive. We didn't get to wrestle on the carpet either, but we did get to sit on the couch every evening with Mom in between us. Sometimes Dad let me lick Kacey's forehead because I loved her so much, and because he thought it was funny when she growled at me.

Not wanting to contribute to the pet overpopulation problem, I agreed to get spayed right after my parents adopted me. I couldn't help but notice a dog wearing a Cone of Shame at the doctor's office. He looked embarrassed, and I felt sorry for him. The nurse explained to me that I would not have to wear a cone as long as I didn't lick my stitches. That sounded like a good deal to me.

I was so tired and sore when I got home from surgery that licking stitches was the last thing on my mind. I went to bed early and felt much better the next day. In fact, I felt good enough to lick my stitches, but I didn't do that because I didn't want to wear a Cone of Shame. As soon as I was fully recovered, Mom gave me some great news: I met all the requirements to help her foster more puppies!

Out in the country, there aren't enough people to give nice homes to all the stray puppies. The lucky ones are rescued by the Nice Lady right before they are euthanized in shelters. They take a car ride into the city, and then go into foster homes like ours until Adoption Day. About 30 puppies from our rescue group get adopted every single week!

Sometimes littermates look very different from each other, and that's because puppies in the same litter can have different fathers. (I bet you didn't know that, but it's true. I know things about dogs.) Sometimes the Nice Lady doesn't know what breed a pup is, so on her website she calls them a "Needahome" pup instead of "Rottweiler mix" or "Shepherd mix." I don't understand why people breed more puppies when thousands of perfectly good ones are killed in shelters every day. It makes me very sad.

Our job as a foster family is to get the pups looking, smelling, and feeling good for Adoption Day. Some of them arrive in bad shape, dehydrated and starving. One puppy was found cuddling against his dead mother on the side of the road. Another pup was scraped off the road by a cleanup crew who thought he was a goner until they felt his faint little heartbeat. He was unconscious, covered in tar and dirt.

When the puppies arrive at our house, they get to eat, drink, and play in the back yard. Then it's time for their first bath. They all have the same stink, and it always makes my dad gag. Some pups try their best to be brave and sit quietly in the tub. Others howl, whine, or try frantically to climb out.

Some of the pups like me right away, but others run away shrieking in terror with tails between their legs. Tiny puppies are very dramatic. I've learned that they warm up to me faster if I lay down instead of stand up, so I do that a lot. When they start to trust me, I trot slowly around the yard carrying a toy low to the ground so they can play with me. Usually I sleep on my doggy bed in my parents' bedroom, but not when we have foster puppies. On those nights, I sleep on the couch downstairs so I can be close to them.

You might think that all puppies have the same personality, but that's not true. Some puppies are so great that Mom cries a little when she takes them to Adoption Day. Other pups are so annoying that we can't wait for them leave. The Nice Lady calls them "Get The Heck Out Of My House" puppies.

Screamy Houdini was a "Get The Heck Out Of My House" puppy. He yelled at the top of his lungs almost constantly and escaped from the puppy pen every 15 seconds. We had another awful puppy that Mom named Cliff, because she wanted to throw him off one. He pooped about 97 times in 3 days.

We fostered a hound puppy with very long ears named Gretel. I was just minding my own business when all of a sudden she started screaming. Mom ran downstairs to scold me for being too rough with her, but then she saw Gretel sitting alone in the middle of the living room—with her ear caught between her own teeth. It's like my dad always says: You can't fix stupid.

Somebody left three puppies in a dumpster to die, so we got to foster them for a few days. Mom named them Chilly, Willy, and Chet. Usually puppies go right to sleep after their first bath, but not these guys. They ran around at warp speed for five hours straight, skidding across our wood floors with toys in their mouths. Now this is just between you and me, but after spending a little time with them, I could see why someone might want to put them in the trash.

Sometimes when Mom and Dad are getting on each other's nerves, they decide to have an "Alone Day" so they don't kill each other. If this happens on a road trip, they draw an invisible line between the driver seat and the passenger seat, and neither is allowed to cross that line. I used that strategy with the dumpster puppies. I understood why they wanted to run around like maniacs, but I needed them to do it away from me. I spent three days enforcing the invisible line between the living room and dining room. I snarled at them when Mom wasn't looking, even though she always tells me to make our guests feel welcome.

As much as Mom and I loved most of the four-legged friends who stayed with us, we were always happy to have the house to ourselves again once they left. After Mom washed the puppy toys and food bowls, we would snuggle on the couch beside Kacey and enjoy the peace and quiet until Dad came home from work. We were very content with our little family, and we didn't need anybody else. Until we met Puppy #245.

21

Squeaker and the Little Huskerd

Her name was Cheyenne, and she was the most beautiful puppy we had ever seen. She was the runt of the litter, only four pounds at ten weeks old. The adorable little Husky Shepherd mix with a velveteen face wiggled her way into our hearts and it quickly became obvious that we couldn't live without her.

Most pups are like little piranhas when they go through the teething stage, so Mom can't hold them very long because they clamp their sharp little teeth on her fingers, ears, and nose. But Cheyenne was different. She sat calmly and quietly in Mom's lap, giving soft sweet kisses instead of chewing her face off. Cheyenne's favorite thing was to cuddle and look deep into Mom's eyes. In our house, this is called "Gaze and Hold."

I had never seen my mom so happy, but I wasn't jealous because I loved the little pup just as much as she did. (Actually I was a little bit jealous that she, at 10 weeks old, was better at climbing stairs than I was.) Whenever Cheyenne took naps on the Winnie the Pooh blanket, I sat down next to the puppy pen and waited for her to wake up. When she was done sleeping, she stood on her little hind legs to smother me with kisses.

When you foster a puppy, you aren't supposed to keep him. You're supposed to take care of him for a few days and then take him to Adoption Day so you can help a different puppy the next week. A lot of volunteers adopt the very first puppy they foster, but my parents had more self-control than that. I was the 56th puppy they fostered; Cheyenne was the 70th. But it doesn't matter whether you adopt the 1st or the 500th puppy; the Nice Lady will wink at you with a smile and call you a "foster failure."

Cheyenne joined our family at the perfect time. Kacey's leg stopped working, so we stopped laughing when she got stuck upside down on the couch. She couldn't happy dance in the yard anymore because she would fall over after a couple of hops. She went to the vet during Senior Pet Month, but he couldn't help her because some things just can't be fixed.

Kacey lost her spunk and seemed a little bit sad, so Mom and Dad knew it was time to do the merciful thing and say goodbye. They loved Kacey as much as anybody could love a rabbit. She had been a major source of laughter and entertainment for over a decade, and it was hard to let her go.

When it was time to put Kacey to sleep, my parents took baby Cheyenne along to make it easier on themselves. Each of them gave Kacey a kiss on the forehead and said their goodbyes. The nurse carried her away in a soft pink blanket. It was a peaceful ending for a crazy, wonderful bunny who lived a long, happy life. Mom hugged on little Cheyenne the whole way home.

Cheyenne was a very low maintenance puppy at first. She held her tiny bladder through most of the night and quietly entertained herself in the morning until the rest of us woke up. A few weeks later she came up with a new routine that focused less on sleep and more on constant togetherness.

At 1:00 AM, she would skip past my doggy bed and cheerfully plant her front paws on Mom's pillow with far more exuberance than was socially acceptable at that time of the morning. Mom always got out of bed, partly because she couldn't resist Cheyenne's big smile, and partly because she wanted to make sure Cheyenne didn't go potty in the house. Once the little pup had successfully recruited Mom, she would pester me with kisses until I was no longer able to ignore her. Then we would walk out to the dark, cold yard and stand there shivering while Cheyenne tried to entice us with her favorite toys.

Eventually we went back inside and slept until she decided she wanted to see us again an hour later. It continued that way through the night until it was time for breakfast, which Cheyenne decided should be at 4:00 AM. Just when we started to hate her a little bit, she would do twirlies all the way from the bedroom to the kitchen. Then she would stop and stare at the food bowls atop the refrigerator. It was very annoying and very cute at the same time. It always took a few minutes to convince her that 4:00 AM was not an acceptable time for breakfast, and then she would go back to sleep for about fifteen minutes before she tried again.

By 6:00 AM we couldn't take it anymore, so Mom told us to Sit and Wait while she poured food into our bowls. Cheyenne always finished her food before I finished mine because my stomach wasn't awake that early. After breakfast, Mom and I would drag our sleepy selves back to bed while Cheyenne occupied her little self by gathering all of the rugs from the house into one big pile. Then she would perch on top of the stack and chew on them a little bit. That's where we found her every morning, sitting on her rug pile with a huge grin on her face.

When Mom took Cheyenne along on trips to the store, people stopped in their tracks when they saw her because she was so darn cute. Grown men lay down on the floor to pet her. I felt proud to be related to her. Sometimes I wished she were a Husky Pug mix so I could tell people that my sister was a "Hug."

Cheyenne was a very mellow love bug who would have been an outstanding therapy dog except for one small problem: she thought everyone was out to kill her. She was highly suspicious of bicyclists, joggers, skateboarders, balloons, flags, beer cans, dishwashers, horses, fire hydrants, road cones, For Sale signs, trash cans, toddlers, and people who hiked without dogs. If we had both worked at Wal-Mart, I would have been the greeter and she would have been a security guard.

At five months old, Cheyenne developed a bark the size of a Tyrannosaurus Rex. One day she barked in the checkout line at the pet store, and a poor little Chihuahua lost control of his bladder. Cheyenne is afraid of a three-hole paper punch, but she will defend Mom with her life.

Luckily Cheyenne decided to let down her guard around little puppies. As soon as she was spayed and vaccinated, Mom started fostering again. Cheyenne was a natural with foster pups, and there was nothing she loved more than having them crawl all over her. Even though she wasn't much older or bigger than our temporary guests, she was very motherly toward them. She even tolerated it when they chewed on her tail or paws.

Cheyenne played the "Good Cop," which forced me to be the "Bad Cop." Somebody had to teach the pups street smarts so they would grow up to have good social skills. I taught them the importance of personal space and the proper way to introduce themselves to another dog. If they happily bounded up to me at full speed, I would roar at them because that kind of disrespectful behavior doesn't fly at places like the dog park. (My roaring scared them, and they always ran to Cheyenne for comfort.) I taught them to approach slowly and then stand still while I sniffed their butts. If they tried to chew on my tail, I engulfed their tiny heads between my jaws. Sure, you judge me—but I probably saved their lives.

Mom invited Grandma for another visit so she could meet her new little granddog. We had a couple of fuzzy, black foster puppies at the same time, and Grandma named them Bear and Chewy. She knelt down in the grass to play with them, and they thought she was the best thing ever. Cheyenne figured if the puppies liked her, then she must be okay. So she plopped down next to Grandma, rolled on her back for a belly rub, and that was that. Grandma was in Cheyenne's very small Circle of Trust.

Not wanting me to feel left out, Grandma took me into the guest room and pulled something out of her suitcase just for me: a fuzzy brown squirrel toy. When I gently lifted it from her hand with my teeth, it squeaked. I knew right then and there that "Squeaker" would be the best toy I would ever have in my entire life. I immediately took it out the doggy door and buried it in the yard so no other dog could steal it from me. That's what you're supposed to do with the very best toys.

22

Valentines and Doorbells

I spend a lot of time wedged between the living room couch and wall because that's the best place to conduct Squirrel Surveillance. Sometimes I'll spend hours there without seeing a single squirrel, but on a good day I might see three squirrels and a cat. When that happens, I have a hard time keeping myself under control. My back legs start to quiver, and I run laps around the house at full speed. I make a weird noise that sounds like someone strangling a goat. One time I even broke a lamp. Sometimes I lose Squirrel Surveillance privileges and Mom shoves the couch close against the wall so I can't see out the window.

There's a saying in Denver that "if you don't like the weather, wait five minutes." So in February when an arctic blast came through Colorado, I waited five minutes. Then I ran back outside and was shocked to find that the weather was still colder than a polar bear's butt. Hundreds of airline flights were cancelled, and a lot of people got in car accidents. Schools were closed for three days because nobody wanted the kids to get frostbite while they were waiting for the bus. Newscasters warned pet owners not to leave their furry friends outside.

I was very thankful that I had a cozy warm house to live in, but those were the most boring three days of my life. I tried to play outside with Cheyenne for a few minutes, but she kept holding up her paws because they hurt from the cold. Mom put my little red booties on her, but that didn't help because I couldn't resist the temptation to yank them right off of her.

On Day 1, Mom pulled the couch out from the wall so we'd have something to do even though I had lost Squirrel Surveillance privileges earlier that week. On Day 2, Dad tried to occupy us with some Doorbell Etiquette Training. If we sat quietly on the rug while he rang the doorbell, then we got treats. We have outstanding Doorbell Etiquette except when we have an actual visitor.

On Day 3, Mom and I decided it would be fun to make some Valentine's Day cards for some elderly folks that I planned to meet the following week. Mom brought out some blank cards and watercolors for me to use. I made pink and purple paw prints on the cards, and then Mom added the words, "I DIG YOU" and "I WUF YOU." Cheyenne didn't make any valentines because she doesn't have any friends (except for foster puppies and Grandma).

The paw prints didn't turn out perfect. In fact some of them smeared so much that you could hardly tell it was my paw print at all. But Mom said not to worry because my friends would love them anyway. She was right.

When we arrived at the group home, a very nice man named Matt smiled and said, "the residents have been asking for you every 30 minutes." We weren't late. They were just excited to see us.

Right away I saw a large ceramic black dog in the corner of the living room. "That's Bruno," Matt explained. "We aren't allowed to have an actual dog live here, so Bruno is as close as we can get." He said they had been on the waiting list for a therapy dog to visit them for over a year, so it was like destiny popped me to them. (They knew I wasn't an official therapy dog yet, but they were happy to help me practice becoming one.) I could have spent all day with Matt because somehow he knew exactly how I loved to be petted. But I was in high demand, so I had to make my rounds.

Matt thought it would be best if I just met a few people at a time. He suggested that we spend a few minutes with the residents in the living room, and then go to the dining room to meet the others. I thought it was a great plan, but the residents in the dining room did not. They couldn't wait to see me, so they wandered in one by one until the lobby was crammed with so many wheelchairs that I could hardly breathe. It was fantastic! They all wanted to pet me, and I wished I were a little taller so they could reach me better.

I could tell from the way Elsie was beaming at me that she was one of the residents who had been asking for me every half hour. She had wavy gray hair and was wearing a pink jogging suit. She was absolutely thrilled with the valentine card I made for her. My mom took a picture of the two of us smiling while Elsie proudly held up her valentine. She had a little trouble remembering my name, so she kept suggesting that I change my name to Lassie. Mom said she could call me whatever she wanted, and that was just fine with me.

Mabel had reddish brown hair, and she was wearing a red robe that was a little too big for her. Mom gave her my valentine card and a red lollipop. Mabel was anxious to taste the treat, so Mom took the plastic wrapper off and gently pushed it into her clenched fist. She happily sucked on it for the remainder of our visit.

Ruth was wearing a pale yellow dress with pretty flowers on it. She had a shiny purple ribbon in her blondish gray hair, and purple nail polish to match. Mom asked if she would like to see me do some tricks, but Ruth was deaf so she just gave us a big toothless grin. I showed her my tricks and she was thoroughly delighted.

Frank, on the other hand, was not as delighted. He opened his valentine without smiling and then inspected his lollipop as if it were a cockroach. He seemed a little bored with my tricks, and then he wheeled himself out of the room. It didn't hurt my feelings at all. Clearly he had something very important to do and I didn't want to keep him from that.

I took myself over to a woman wearing eyeglasses and a black headband. She had a zebra-striped blanket on her lap. When I gave her the valentine I had made, she said in a serious tone, "I had no idea an animal could do such a thing." She told me that she used to have a pet Chihuahua, and I could tell she had loved him with all her heart. She had grown up in an orphanage and loved to sing, so I decided her name should be Annie.

Just then Annie wanted me to come close enough for petting, so she yelled something at me and then nearly strangled me with the leash. I didn't mind. She kept asking me to Speak but I hadn't learned that trick yet so I shook her hand instead.

At 4:00 PM, it was time for us to leave so they could get ready to eat dinner. Annie pulled me aside and said she would really like to sing a song for me next the time I came. I wondered if she would sing *Tomorrow* or *It's a Hard Knock Life*. Whatever she chose, I was sure it would be fantastic.

I went back to visit my friends a couple of months later. As soon as we got there, Elsie exclaimed, "I still have the valentine you gave me!" Ruth was wearing a tiara for no reason, and I thought she looked beautiful. Annie sang not just one but TWO songs. I had never heard them before, but I thought they were quite pretty.

I looked around and noticed Mabel wasn't there. Matt told me that she passed away a few days after my last visit. I was sad because I hardly got to know her, but at least I had the opportunity to meet her before she was gone. I would always remember watching her smile as she held that red lollipop.

23

Bear Bells and Rednecks

That following summer was amazing because Mom found a library book listing all the best places to go hiking and camping with dogs. We started with all the places that were rated "4 Wags" because that was the best ranking possible. We began in early June, when little patches of snow were still on the ground in the mountains. We saw marmots, chipmunks, deer, moose, and SQUIRRELS. We kept on exploring throughout late summer—when it was too hot to stay at our house in the suburbs. Mom liked September the best because the aspen leaves were bright yellow and orange. She took five million pictures and made us stop to pose for most of them, which was pretty annoying. We hiked until the snow started falling again in mid-October.

My parents have been married 18 years and they are still in love. It's quite sickening, and perhaps you'll be glad to know they don't always get along swell. They argue whenever they drive, paint a room, do their taxes, or pack for a camping trip. Dad likes to take as few things as possible. He thinks camping should be like it was when he was in junior high: hike to a rugged tent site with everything you need strapped to your back.

Mom likes to take as many things as possible, and she likes to park right next to a well-groomed tent site located near an outhouse (to lessen the chance of bears chasing her on midnight potty runs). Dad can get his stuff ready in 10 minutes, which leaves him 30 minutes to complain about how long it takes Mom to gather her things, the dog stuff, and all the food. Once my mom gives my dad the okay to load everything into the truck, he mutters things under his breath like, "Why in the heck do we have so much junk?" and "We need a bigger truck."

Just when it's finally time to start the drive to the mountains, Mom says she will die unless she has some breakfast and that's when smoke starts shooting out of Dad's nostrils. (Mom is hypoglycemic, which means that she turns into a horrible person if she doesn't eat something every two hours.)

Eventually everybody is loaded into the truck with full bellies and empty bladders. After about 30 minutes, Mom breaks the angry silence by saying, "You are driving way too fast on these narrow mountain roads." Dad reaches over and turns up the volume on the radio. Some married couples claim that they never fight. My parents are not one of those couples.

Cheyenne threw up on the way to her very first camping trip because Mom was playing a John Denver CD. As soon as we got to the campground, the fighting and nausea came to an abrupt end. We couldn't help but get along with each other because the Rocky Mountains were so beautiful. Pine trees surrounded us and smelled wonderful. Dad found a perfect little campsite with a creek running beside it. He set up the tent, and then Mom filled it with air mattresses, sleeping bags, and pillows.

We decided to go on a short hike since we still had plenty of daylight. So we took everything out of the truck and strapped most of it to our backs because hiking is serious business in Colorado. You can't just scale a mountain wearing a T-shirt and cowboy boots like my dad's redneck friend Chip tried to do. There are afternoon thunderstorms, wild animals, and subzero temperatures at night. You've got to be prepared. You've got to have a system. You've got to have a plan.

Mom told a friend where we were going and what time we planned to be back. Dad marked what time we left to make sure we returned before dark. He wore a pack full of water, warm clothes, a compass, knife, and first aid kit for humans. Mom carried an asthma inhaler, chapstick, hand sanitizer, a camera, Kleenex, water, granola bars, bear bells, a cell phone, a whistle, waterproof matches, an emergency blanket, a rain poncho, sunscreen, mosquito repellent, and a first aid kit for dogs.

I wore my very own pack because it made me look cool. I carried dog food, water bottles, a collapsible yellow water bowl, and poop bags. Cheyenne wore a pack too, but it was empty because she was just a little pup in training. Mom tied bright orange bandanas around our necks so we'd be easy to spot in the woods.

We didn't wear leashes because we don't have to in the national forest. Cheyenne never strayed far, unlike most Huskies. She stuck to Mom like Velcro. I kept an eye out for squirrels while Mom kept an eye out for bears and mountain lions. Cheyenne and I jumped through patches of snow and took a quick dip in a mountain stream.

Mom took pictures of flowers, trees, mountains, and us. (Cheyenne and I are trained to look at her whenever she says, "Eyes." Sometimes we pretend to forget what that command means when we are tired of posing for pictures.) After a while we got hungry and tired so we headed back to camp. Dad always knows his way back. He has superior navigational skills, which is one of the reasons Mom married him. She is literally lost without him.

Dad built a warm campfire, and Mom cooked pizza mountain pies. She spread a dog blanket out for Cheyenne and me, and then gave us toys filled with peanut butter. When we were finished with dessert, Mom sat down beside us and played the guitar. Cheyenne drifted off to sleep with her chin on Mom's lap, and I gazed up at the beautiful bright stars.

That's how it was for the whole summer and fall. We were the luckiest dogs on the planet. Whenever my parents had a day off, we headed to another exciting place in the dog book. We didn't always go camping. Sometimes we just went for a day hike or tried out a new dog park.

Cheyenne and I quickly learned to recognize the early signs of upcoming fun. Our morning routine was to sit side by side with eager anticipation to see which clothes Mom would pull out of the closet. We knew which ones were the Fun Pants, and Cheyenne always squealed with delight when Mom chose those. Cheyenne squealed again whenever Mom grabbed thick hiking socks instead of the boring white ones. Even I couldn't contain my excitement when Mom laced up her hiking boots.

My parents learned everything they possibly could about dogs before they adopted Cheyenne and me. They watched TV shows and read several books about canine behavior. They figured if they educated themselves as much as possible, we would turn out perfect. They were wrong. My parents were only dog experts until they got actual dogs.

Perfect pooches only exist in the movies but mom didn't know that, so she lay awake at night trying to figure out what she did wrong. Eventually she realized that none of her friends had perfect dogs either. They dug under or jumped over their fences. They were terrified to ride in the car, and they seized every opportunity to dart out the front door. They drank from the toilet and stole things out of the kitchen trash. I have never done any of those things.

I do, however, have trouble sitting still when my parents try to snap my collar on because I am so excited to go on a walk. My parents go out of their way to put our leashes on quietly so we will stay calm instead of acting like maniacs, but my legs quiver and I can't help but pace around the living room. Cheyenne completely loses her mind. Sometimes Mom and Dad wish they had just gotten an ant farm or some sea monkeys.

Cheyenne and I aren't allowed to go out the front door until we Sit and Wait so we can start the walk in a focused, obedient manner. But no matter how many hundreds of times our parents have practiced this, the moment they say Okay, all hell breaks loose. (I'm not allowed to say *hell*.) Cheyenne pulls as though she is a champion sled dog and I dart around looking for squirrels. We get tangled up and Mom says bad words. Dad says it's like walking a couple of yo-yos. My parents have tried a thousand different approaches to get us to walk beside them calmly in a straight line, but nothing seems to work so they take us places where we can have off-leash fun whenever possible.

We spent one day at a dog agility course, and I don't mean to brag but Cheyenne and I were the smartest dogs there. Dad used treats to lure us up and down the ramp and through the tube. Other dog owners were impressed and a little bit jealous. One man complained because his dog wasn't interested in the obstacle course. I'm pretty sure he would have had more success if he had brought treats for his four-legged failure.

Just when we started to get a little bored, Cheyenne and I spotted some grasshoppers. I'm not talking about three or four grasshoppers. I'm talking about gazillions. We pounced on them for an hour while Mom giggled.

We ended the very fun day by goofing around at a doggy beach. I splashed through the water while Cheyenne tried to bite the little waves. Mom and Dad enjoyed the mountain scenery, and we played until we were covered with sand from head to toe.

Dad decided to take all of us fishing one day, so we got all of our stuff together and off we went. We had to hike to the fishing spot on a beautiful trail, so Mom had no choice but to take a lot of pictures. Dad wore his Indiana Jones hat because Mom thinks it makes him look extra handsome. I hiked through purple wildflowers that were taller than me.

We reached the river after an hour or so. Cheyenne and I jumped from rock to rock like gazelles while Dad unloaded his fishing gear from his gigantic red backpack. He pulled out his fishing license, wading pants, wading boots, bait, hooks, and fishing line. He had everything he needed except for one thing: a fishing pole. Oops. (Dad never forgot his fishing pole again after that, but he did forget bait.)

We made the best of it and spent some time playing, resting, and eating snacks. Then Dad put on his heavy pack again, and we headed back down the trail. Things were going pretty well until some horses ran up behind us at 90 miles an hour. I barely had time to hurl myself into the bushes. I don't like horses—on TV or in real life. Their big bulging eyes give me the creeps.

All of us survived that hiking season, probably because of Mom's strong commitment to bear bells. I couldn't wait to do the same thing again next year.

24

Peanuts and the Test

Some folks spend hundreds of dollars to pay a professional to train their pooch to become a certified therapy dog. My mom is not one of those people; she is a penny-pincher. She used the Internet to find out what I needed to know, and then she trained me herself.

You're probably wondering if there's a difference between a therapy dog and a service dog, and the answer is yes. Rocco, for example, is a service dog for a little girl named Suzie. Suzie has a peanut allergy so severe that if she walks into a room that has a peanut shell, her throat will close up and she'll stop breathing if she doesn't get medical help immediately. Rocco has been trained to alert Suzie whenever he smells a peanut. He is very smart and disciplined. If he were to see a squirrel holding a peanut, he would keep his focus, alert Suzie and escort her to a safe distance. By comparison, if a therapy dog such as myself were to see a squirrel holding a peanut, I would ditch Suzie and devour the squirrel. Then I would eat the peanut for dessert. I can't speak for all therapy dogs, of course, but that's what I would do. Some service dogs are worth $30,000 or more, whereas I'd probably only go for about $25 on eBay.

I was shopping one day with my mom at a camping store when I met a yellow Lab puppy named Buster. He was there with a five-year-old boy named Steven who had epilepsy. Buster was training to become Steven's very own service dog so he could bark whenever Steven was about to have a seizure, and then lie down next to him so he wouldn't get hurt.

Service dogs are amazing, and I'd probably be jealous if I didn't admire them so much. They can alert a deaf person to the sound of a doorbell, telephone, alarm clock, or smoke alarm. They can remind people with mental disabilities to take their medicine. They can help soldiers with post-traumatic stress disorder by steering them away from a stressful situation. Some diabetics have service dogs who can detect when their blood sugar level is getting too low.

I suppose you could say that a service dog focuses on making things easier for people, whereas a therapy dog focuses on making them happier. For example, I can't open a refrigerator door or turn on a light for a disabled war veteran, but I can give him a High Five if he's feeling down in the dumps. I can't help a blind woman cross the street, but I can cuddle next to her while she tells me about her day.

A therapy dog brings joy and comfort to people in hospitals, retirement homes, nursing homes, schools, and disaster areas. He has to be patient, gentle, and friendly toward kids and adults. He must be comfortable around people with unusual styles of walking, moving, or breathing. There's a saying that "a therapy dog is born, not made." That's because you can't change a dog's inherent temperament; either they enjoy interacting with strangers or they don't.

After several months of meeting new friends at stores, nursing homes, and homeless shelters, Mom thought I was ready to take the test to become an official, certified therapy dog. She figured it might take a couple of attempts, so there was no pressure on either of us. We decided to give it a try and then keep working on whichever areas needed improvement.

We took a long, scenic drive together that day. We were a little bit nervous about taking the test until my theme song came on the radio: "Let My Love Open The Door." When Mom and I heard it, we relaxed and remembered why we were taking the test in the first place. It was so we could find more people to love.

We arrived early and decided to keep calm by going on a walk around the neighborhood. Mom said she was proud of me no matter what happened, and then we headed inside. The instructor waved to us from the back of the pet store. Several other dogs were patiently waiting with their owners. Mom and I watched them take the test, and then it was our turn.

The test evaluator's name was Helen, and I liked her right away. I sat politely while she talked to my mom and then reached down to pet me. She said I looked and smelled nice, and just like that, I had passed the first three sections of the test. Then Helen asked my mom to walk me around the room on a loose leash. I had to turn left, right, and stop whenever Mom did. We maneuvered around a few people and their dogs. My mom steered me through an obstacle course of toys on the ground and told me to Leave It whenever I started to lick one. (I think the purpose of that was to prove that I wouldn't eat pills on the floor at a hospital.) Mom smiled at me. We were doing great so far.

Mom told me to Sit and Stay. She walked 10 feet away and then told me to Come. No problem. Then she left me with Helen for a few minutes while she left the room. I didn't freak out, so that was one more check on the list of test requirements. Helen dropped a large book on the floor behind me. The sound scared me a little bit, but I remained composed. Then she tried to see if I'd panic when she hunched over me while using a walker. I was cool as a cucumber, and I could tell she was impressed. Mom winked at me.

The last section of the test was a challenge, and I didn't get it perfect. I was supposed to sit quietly while Mom talked to a stranger. Helen explained the purpose was to practice minding my own business when Mom met people who didn't like dogs. I thought I must have heard her wrong because I couldn't imagine anyone not liking a dog. So when Mom greeted the stranger, I did too.

When the test was over, Helen asked us to sit down next to the other dogs and their owners. Mom and I were proud of each other, even though we made a few little mistakes here and there. We tried to remember there was no pressure to pass this time and that we were just trying to figure out which skills we needed to improve. Still, we were a little bit nervous and hoped for a good score.

Helen called each "team" up one at a time, and we all rooted for each other while she announced whether or not we passed. First there was a Labradoodle named Clyde. His parents were hoping to start taking him to schools so he could help children overcome reading disabilities. All of us cheered when he got Helen's stamp of approval. Next there was a little Beagle named Willie. His mom was hoping to take him to a shelter for abused women and children. Willie passed too, and everybody clapped for him. A few more dogs passed with flying colors: a Greyhound, a German Shepherd mix, and a Golden Retriever. Finally it was my turn. Mom crossed her fingers. It seemed like an eternity until Helen smiled and congratulated us. We couldn't believe it. We passed on our very first try!

We didn't stop smiling the whole way home. Dad greeted us with High Fives and said we were very Good Girls. I don't think he had ever been more proud of my mom and me. He bragged about us to all of his friends, and we felt like a million bucks.

All of our training had not been in vain. We were officially certified to spend the rest of our lives making a difference. We were on a mission to find all sorts of people to love… a sick child who needed a hug… a lonely veteran waiting for a friend. Destiny had brought Mom and me together. We were a terrific team, and we were ready to change the world.

25

Fireworks and Spitting in Holes

I failed out of the therapy dog program almost immediately. Well, actually I didn't actually "fail" out of the program *per se*. Nobody insisted that I had to leave; Mom just decided that perhaps it wasn't my destiny to be a therapy dog after all. It just so happened that right after I earned my certification, I hit puberty. I bet you didn't know that dogs could go through a rebellious teenager stage, but it's true.

I shoplifted treats from a pet store, ate three Mountain Dew cans, and threw up a firework. I started burping loudly in public and set a very poor example for Cheyenne. I barked at homeless children and little old ladies.

Some days I woke up and felt like chasing a squirrel instead of comforting my disabled friends. Sometimes I wanted to be alone instead of letting elderly folks pet me. Mom was disappointed, but she didn't pressure me to be something I wasn't. She loved me just the way I was, therapy dog dropout and all. She knew what it was like to go through adolescence because she had been there herself.

My mom threw ice cream at an old lady when she was in high school. (It was an accident, but she still feels terrible about it.) Grandma blamed herself for the teenage rebellion because she had not put my mom in the GATE (Gifted and Talented Education) program in junior high. She had feared that my mom would start thinking she was better than the other kids. So instead of reaping the benefits of higher learning, my mom started sniffing White Out and spitting into holes at the miniature golf course. My grandma has never forgiven herself.

I became a bully at the dog park, so my mom stopped taking me there for a while. During that time, my only friend (besides Cheyenne) was a Rat Terrier mix named Sammy. Neither of our parents let us play together because both of us had behavioral problems. He liked to pick fights with big dogs because he didn't realize he was small. His parents looked into finding him professional help, and last I heard they were planning to enroll him in a Grumpy Growlers class. Sammy and I e-mailed regularly to keep in touch, but that grew boring after a while. I needed more than one four-legged friend so I finally admitted that I had a problem and agreed to get help.

My parents decided that Cheyenne and I should spend some time at a doggy dude ranch in order to improve our social skills. It was out in the middle of nowhere, which is exactly where a dude ranch should be. You have to follow a dirt road past a peaceful cemetery with a big shade tree. Depending on the weather, sometimes you can see bright colored hot air balloons floating in the sky. We turned into the driveway when we spotted the big barn with two red doors. We were greeted by some chickens and a couple of goats, which Mom said were for "looking at" and not for "eating."

Mom told the lady we were there because we were socially challenged. She paid in advance for a package deal because she thought she would save a lot of money. However she is bad at mental math, so really she only saved five bucks (one of many tragic results of the infamous GATE program decision).

The dude ranch wasn't as big as our neighborhood dog park, so we had to be on our best behavior since we were stuck with the other dogs all day. I knew that if I started a fight, then I would eventually have to apologize and work things out. I figured it would be easier and less embarrassing just to relax and have fun, so that's what I did.

I met a nice dog named Xandra whose parents took her there so she could hang out with her furry friends instead of being stuck in a crate all day while they were at work. I wrestled with Junior, a Golden Retriever who was there because his owners were too old to take him on long walks. I played chase with a mutt named Murray who was trying to overcome separation anxiety whenever his parents went on vacation.

When it got too hot to play in the sunshine, I either took myself inside the barn via the doggy door or I rested under a shade tree. I didn't have the courage to cool off in the plastic kiddie pool, but it was fun to watch a couple of Labrador Retrievers splash around. I loved it there, and I could have stayed forever.

Cheyenne absolutely hated the dude ranch. She spent the entire day nervously pacing around the perimeter with her tail between her legs. She did everything in her power to avoid contact with all of the other dogs. The staff was friendly, but she wouldn't let any of them pet her. It was embarrassing. I kept my distance so no one would know she was my sister.

At the end of the day, Cheyenne was so relieved to see Mom that she threw up. The lady told her that I had behaved perfectly and didn't try to bully anybody. I don't mean to brag, but I'm pretty sure I was the best dog there. Cheyenne and I slept the whole way home. I was physically exhausted from playing, and Cheyenne was emotionally drained from defending her personal space.

26

Batgirl and Red Dresses

I figured I'd have some extra time to hone in on my Squirrel Surveillance skills after I dropped out of the therapy dog program, but Mom had other plans for me. The dude ranch helped me improve my social skills with other dogs, but Mom decided it would be best if I loved people from a distance while I went through my adolescent stage. She figured there had to be something I could do to help others even if I couldn't visit homeless shelters or nursing homes.

Right about that time, a couple of guys from my dad's flag football team told her about a little girl with the number #146 pinned to her shirt. This child spent every evening locked in a room with several other girls, all of whom wore red dresses. They watched cartoons while men stared at them through a pane of glass—and then ordered them by number as if they were fast food items. Sometimes they were sold 15 times per night.

This bothered my mom a whole lot, and she was never the same after that. She decided to spend the rest of her life trying to help those little girls, as if they were her own children. She lay awake at night trying to figure out what we could do, and that's when she got an idea.

Normal people bake goodies or run a 5K when they want to raise money for a cause they are passionate about. But my mom isn't normal. She wanted to do something funny and unusual— something that would get people talking about the uncomfortable subject of child trafficking. So she decided to do a Stupid-a-thon. Usually she does stupid things for free (like walking into the Men's Restroom at the airport or using carpet cleaner to remove a shadow off of the floor), but that month she decided to charge people. She asked friends and family to come up with stupid things for her to do, and then she did those stupid things to earn their donation.

Mom's old college buddy promised to donate money if she wore a cape and rode her bike off of a jump. So Dad built a ramp in front of our house. Mom put on a motorcycle helmet and pushed aside her high school memory of crashing a bike in front of the school bus. Cheyenne and I sat on the sidewalk with eager anticipation while Mom stuck her wet finger in the air to test the direction of the wind. A young neighbor girl came over for moral support, and Dad held the video camera. Curious strangers drove by in vans, and embarrassed neighbors hid inside their houses.

Mom slowly mounted the bicycle with the skill of an arthritic elderly woman. She started out wobbly, then gained some momentum… and made it! Mom squealed with relief, and Dad whooped and hollered for her. Cheyenne and I were very impressed, so we stood on our hind legs and gave her several High Fives.

Another friend promised to make a donation if Mom would go Christmas Caroling in May. So she put on some tall, red socks and a big, bright elf hat with bells. She sang *Rudolph the Red Nosed Reindeer* at the first house, and was relieved when the couple sang along so she wouldn't feel quite so dumb. Next she sang *Jingle Bells* for two teenage girls who were visibly embarrassed for her. Mom's favorite house was the last one. She belted out *We Wish You A Merry Christmas* to a dog and two dancing five-year-olds.

Grandma made a donation after my mom did a photo shoot called "America's Next Top Moron." Mom crafted a spectacularly hideous dress out of black trash bags and silver duct tape. She tucked a tall plastic cup in her hair so it would stick straight up on her head. Then she found an empty lot and lay down in the dirt. Mom's good friend Naomi took photos of her glaring at the camera with angry expressions. Next Mom put on a high quality gown made of green bubble wrap and climbed into a big black garbage can. Naomi took pictures of her peeking out of it while they both tried to not to giggle.

My mom earned her next donation by spending a day at the mall with a large, black, curly mustache drawn above her lips. Loyal Naomi followed along with the video camera as Mom tried on sunglasses and bought a snack at the food court. Teenage girls glared as my mom posed next to mannequins and twirled through a clothing store. She received twice the donation that was promised after posting a video of her humiliating day to the tune of *I Feel Pretty*.

Mom wanted me to go trick-or-treating with her in June, but I was pretty busy with Squirrel Surveillance and also I didn't have a costume. She couldn't believe how hard it was to get neighbors to answer their doorbell for Batgirl in the springtime. Nobody gave her any candy, but she did manage to bring home a dog treat, a package of hot dogs, and some ranch dressing.

Friends and family came up with all sorts of fun challenges and donated hundreds of dollars. Her Stupid-a-thon was a huge success and the money helped to build a safe home for victims as young as six years old. Most of the girls in red dresses were rescued during a raid on that brothel, but Number 146 was no longer there. We don't know what happened to her, but she isn't forgotten. She is a constant reminder of the many children who still need help.

27

Princess Dresses and Dogfights

Dad racked his brain for weeks trying to think of a way to make Mom's 40th birthday special. She asked him for the gift of "fat," so she could spend the rest of her life eating whatever she wanted without worrying if he would stop loving her. Dad didn't like that idea, so he came up with a plan to have a Princess Party in hopes that she would finally stop complaining that no one had ever given her a tiara.

Mom was delighted with the idea. She shopped at thrift stores all over town until she found the perfect pink princess gown. I could tell it was a high quality item because of all the fake diamonds glued to it. She bought a candy necklace and matching bracelet.

Pink invitations were sent out with fancy handwriting that read, "Hear Ye, Hear Ye! All princesses across the land are invited to attend a royal party." Mom thinks it's a shame that most people have to wait until they die before their friends will travel across the country to visit, so she tried to push the idea of a Pre-Funeral Princess Party. She offered distant friends a written release of obligation to attend her future funeral, but none of them took the bait.

On the day of the party, Dad surprised Mom with a dozen roses. He said it took a long time to decide which colors she would like best, and in the end he chose the ones that would be the prettiest with her dress. She got tears in her eyes and gave him a kiss on the cheek. Then they hung a big pink banner in the front window that said "Princess Party."

I ate a dead mouse right before all of Mom's girlfriends showed up wearing their old prom dresses. She gave each of them a beautiful tiara from the dollar store. They giggled a lot, played *Pin the Kiss on the Frog*, and drew pictures of dragons onto paper plates perched atop their heads. Then they drank grape soda and competed for prizes in a very unladylike burping contest. Princess Renee won a Cinderella yo-yo, and Princess Naomi won a Sleeping Beauty coloring book.

Mom was having a fantastic time until I beat up Cheyenne in the back yard. She was very angry when she had to march outside in her princess gown to referee our fight over a new toy that she had specifically bought to entertain us during the party. I had never been in a fight with Cheyenne before, and Mom said my timing was lousy. She used that opportunity for a Teaching Moment and told me, "Everybody makes mistakes and that's okay, but it's important to apologize." I didn't understand exactly what she said because I'm just a dog, but I could tell she was disappointed in me. I hung my head and gave Cheyenne a kiss. She knew I was sorry, so she went back inside to enjoy the rest of her celebration.

The party guests sang *Happy Birthday* and then ate a princess cake with pink frosting on purple plates. Instead of bringing gifts, they dropped money into a little box for Mom's favorite charity that read, "Thank you for helping other little princesses!" (Their donations were used to buy princess dresses for some little girls in a safe home.)

At sunset, the Royal Ball began and the silly princesses did the Hokey Pokey and danced to the tune of *Once Upon A Dream* (the theme to *Sleeping Beauty*). The party was perfect, and Mom would always remember it as a very fun day spent with people she loved.

After all of the guests went home, Dad handed Mom a gift-wrapped box. She had only asked for one present: a distress beacon. With just a push of a button, Mom would now be able to summon forest rangers to rescue us if we got hurt or lost on a mountain hike. She thought it was the best invention in the history of the world. Dad couldn't think of anything more stupid to spend hard-earned money on. They had argued about it for months because married people are legally obligated to have different opinions about how to spend their money. In the end, he bought it because he's crazy about her.

28

Swim Goggles and Dolly Parton

Date Day is kind of a big deal at our house. When it's my dad's turn to choose, my parents usually go see a superhero movie at the theater. But when it's my mom's turn to choose, things tend to spiral out of control. Dad says she's always coming up with ideas that could get them arrested.

Mom's ideas usually work well on a tight budget. Sometimes she just wants to slow dance in the living room with the lights dimmed enough to be romantic, but not so much that she can't see Dad in all of his handsomeness. Sometimes she likes to sit on the couch and look through photo albums. She thinks more people would stay married if they looked at old photos together and realized how much they had been through together. When I look at the photo of Dad wearing a cowboy hat and Mom wearing a bunch of green balloons pinned to her overalls, I just see a silly picture of them at a Halloween party. But when my parents look at that same photo, they see a memory of a woman dressed in a red devil outfit who whispered, "That cowboy sure is sexy" –and the response by the host of the party: "He's off limits. He's married to the grapes."

Mom's very favorite thing to do on Date Day is make funny videos. Dad was worried they would attract the local police when they dressed up as Scrabble tiles before Halloween and danced around the local business park. Mom set the video camera on a small tri-pod and giggled when people hurried past, afraid to make eye contact. My dad was the letter "I" and Mom was "U." The finished corny video was set to a sappy music medley of *I Can't Smile Without U, Just U and I*, and *I Will Always Love U*.

A few weeks later, Mom got a hankering to do a video of *Beat It* by Michael Jackson, so Dad put on a white glittery glove and moon danced across the living room. I let him borrow my spiked collar so he would look really tough like the guys in the actual video. Next they dressed up like zombies and dragged themselves around the house for the song *Thriller*. I didn't recognize my mom when she came downstairs, so I initiated the Emergency Barking System. That was when I learned how terrifying zombies could be, and I was very relieved when she took off the scary makeup.

When one of Dad's friends saw the Michael Jackson video, he requested that my folks make a video imitating popular bands throughout music history. Dad said there was no way he would ever do that, but in the end all Mom had to do was bribe him with a new video game. She bought a second video game just to make sure he participated cheerfully.

They stayed awake until the wee hours of the morning giggling at music videos on the Internet, trying to decide which ones would be the most fun to imitate. Mom gathered wigs and costumes from family, friends, thrift stores, and party stores.

Dad swayed his hips and lip-synched *Heartbreak Hotel* into a mop handle. Then they put on matching wigs, suits, and electric guitars. Mom knew all the words to *Can't Buy Me Love*, but Dad just bobbed his head back and forth in true Beatles fashion. They tied plastic cereal bowls to their heads when it was time to impersonate Devo. As if black muscle shirts with tall black socks weren't hideous enough, Mom wore the bright red swim goggles that she uses to slice onions. She used a TV tray in place of a keyboard, and I was embarrassed to call her my mother.

Mom thought Dad's knees looked sexy when he wore a cheerleader outfit for the song *Mickey*. I was very impressed with how well he memorized the cheerleader routine. Mom stuffed balloons under her shirt and wore fake eyelashes for the next song, but Dad's "Kenny Rogers" wig wasn't quite right so friends thought they were Dolly Parton and Moses.

I could tell Cheyenne was impressed with their performances of Twisted Sister, Prince, and New Kids on the Block. Mom giggled when Dad put on a blond Madonna wig and strapped silver party hats to his chest. Next they wore black dresses to perform as Wilson Phillips, even though they lacked a third person to help them *Hold On* for one more day. When it was time to be Celine Dion, Mom put on her beloved princess gown and dimmed the lights. Dad aimed the hairdryer so it looked like she was at the bow of a ship on a windy day.

A friend said Mom made a better Justin Bieber than the real one, but I've seen him on TV and he seems pretty great. It does make sense though, that someone would say she does a good impression of a teenage boy because everyone thought she *was* one until college.

Mom's friend Joyce showed the video to her father, and he asked if my parents were on drugs. She assured him that they were not, and they were just two people in love who liked to make others laugh. Another friend watched the video and said my folks had too much time on their hands. Mom knew that wasn't true because it's never a waste of time to laugh with your husband. Days like that make life worth living.

29

Chicken Soup and Mice Heroes

Sometimes I avoid bedtime, even when I'm exhausted, because I don't want to miss out on anything fun. My usual routine is to wander around aimlessly with droopy eyes until my parents tuck me in. They bend down, kiss me on my forehead, and whisper "Good Girl." Sometimes they even sing to me. I love it, but sometimes I worry that other dogs will find out and I'll lose my street credit.

One night I had to tuck myself into bed because Mom was sick with a cold. Dad was at work when he found out, so he stopped on his way home and surprised her with some pink roses that made her cry. Even though she "smelled like death," he took very good care of her because of The Marriage Pact (an agreement they made as newlyweds to take extra good care of each other when they were sick). So instead of getting annoyed with her for being useless, he said things like, "You poor thing" and made chicken noodle soup.

Mom was sick for two long weeks, so Cheyenne and I didn't get to go out for walks like we usually do. Mostly we just sat around and listened to her blow her nose. It was horrible for us. My parents have a collection of Disney movies that they watch whenever they are sick. I cuddled with Mom on the couch and we watched *The Rescuers*, which is her favorite movie in the whole wide world. It's about two little mice who rescue a little orphan girl named Penny. I had never seen the movie before, and it left me feeling very inspired. After all, if two tiny mice could find a way to help a child in need, then surely I could too.

Right around the time Mom started to feel better, she heard that a friend was planning to visit some children who had been rescued and didn't have to wear numbers on their shirts anymore. Mom got a great idea for raising money to rescue more kids, so she gave her friend some paper, colored pencils, and a picture of the two of us. We waited patiently for him to return from the safe home, and that was hard to do because we were very excited.

A few weeks later he came back with the most wonderful drawings I had ever seen. The kids had drawn colorful pictures of butterflies, flowers, smiling clouds, and sunshine. One drawing in particular was my favorite because it was a dog. Or possibly a rabbit. Maybe a kangaroo. The exact details don't matter because, in my heart, I know it was a dog. And I'm pretty sure that dog was me.

Mom figured out a way to transfer that artwork onto unfinished wooden Christmas ornaments, and Grandma flew in from California to help. They went to practically every craft store in the whole state and bought gobs of unfinished ornaments shaped like hearts, butterflies, and—to surprise me—dogs! Dad drilled holes in the wood and sanded the edges down smooth. Grandma did the painting, and Mom attached the artwork with decoupage glue.

Mom thought her friends who like dogs might want to buy heart-shaped ornaments with my paw print, so I put my best paw forward. We sold 200 ornaments that first year, and the money helped to prevent children from being sold into the sex trade.

30

Apple Pie and Thumping Tails

By the time my parents were ready to celebrate their 18th wedding anniversary, Mom had decided she was too old to enjoy tent camping anymore. She wanted a toilet she could find in the middle of the night without having to walk through a dark, scary forest. It was a reasonable request, so Dad found a perfect place to take her.

When we arrived at the ranch in the mountains, a woman named Kathy greeted us with a big smile and two slices of homemade apple pie. She said the other guests had postponed their reservations, so we had the whole place to ourselves. I was pretty sure she said Cheyenne and I could run around the whole time without our leashes, but just then I saw a chipmunk run past our truck and dart into a hole. My dad had left the rear window down in the 4Runner because he knew it would never cross my mind to jump out. I had received high quality car etiquette training for more than two years. I was self-disciplined. I was obedient. I was not allowed to exit a vehicle unless my parents said Okay.

Kathy stood beside the truck and pointed toward the cabin we reserved. At that very moment, I gracefully catapulted myself out of the truck and raced with squealing excitement to the chipmunk's hole. The peaceful mountain silence was shattered, and Mom screamed at me in such a way that I knew I was a huge embarrassing failure. Dad was relieved when Kathy didn't ask us to leave right then and there.

The little wooden hunter's cabin looked like it might collapse at any moment, but it was clean and the mountain views were spectacular. A chalkboard sign hung right out front with the words "Welcome Jeff and Michelle, 1st Guests of Summer 2012." The cabin was nestled in pine trees, and there was a creek just a stone's throw away from the front porch.

Mom was so overwhelmed with the beautiful scenery that she could not focus on doing anything useful. She just wandered around aimlessly until Dad finally got impatient and made her help unload the truck. Mom filled the little refrigerator with food that she had prepared earlier in the week so she could spend the weekend relaxing instead of cooking.

I explored the cabin and was delighted to find so many spiders in the tiny bathroom. They looked delicious, but I didn't have time to snack on them right then because I wanted to do some exploring outside before sunset. A squirrel was chattering behind the cabin, so I darted through the forest in an attempt to catch him. I came back empty-handed with a big stick caught in my collar. My parents laughed at me, and Cheyenne was glad I didn't get hurt.

Dad built a warm campfire and roasted some hot dogs. Mom played the guitar until Cheyenne and I were too sleepy to keep our eyes open. They tucked us into our doggy beds, and we dreamed about how much fun we would have the next day.

At 6:30 AM the next morning, Cheyenne and I stood beside our parents' bed to offer a cheerful greeting—and that's why it's a bad idea to bring pets on a relaxing, romantic vacation. Mom heated up some breakfast casserole while Dad took us to play in the creek. We rolled around in reddish muddy clay and got so dirty that Mom refused to let us back into the cabin until bedtime.

The weather was perfect. Dad decided it was more important to have happy dogs than catch a fish, so he let us play in the water even though we scared the fish away. (Truth be told, he's not a very good fisherman. One time he hooked his own butt.) Cheyenne was content to sit and watch him fish for hours, but I didn't have the patience for that so I spent my time feverishly digging for critters until my nose was raw. Then I dug some more. It was the best day of my life.

Dad can always tell how happy Mom is by how many pictures she takes. She used up an entire memory card and drained two batteries within 24 hours. She took pictures of all the same stuff she usually does (mountains, trees, and flowers), plus some of Dad fishing and me digging.

Later that afternoon my folks played cribbage and ate brownies while Cheyenne took a nap and I continued to dig for critters. Dad didn't catch any fish that day, but he was happy just the same. That night you could see a gazillion stars shining brightly in the sky, but Mom and Dad didn't dare spend too much time gazing at them because Kathy had warned that a bear liked to wander around after dark.

Early the next morning, Mom and Dad woke up to the sound of two tails thumping against the wall. Cheyenne and I were ready to start our day, and we couldn't figure out how to get our hiking packs on by ourselves. We found a trail that circled a beautiful lake. We saw marmots and a few elk, but no bears. Mom got her shoelace caught on a tree branch and fell down because bad luck follows her everywhere. When we got to an open meadow of yellow wildflowers, Dad twirled around like he was in *The Sound of Music* just to make us laugh. Mom got a bug stuck under her eyelid, and then we stopped for a late picnic lunch. We noticed some smoke off in the distance but didn't think much of it.

On our way back to the cabin, we met the ranch hand and he was very nice. He had a gray beard and talked real slow the way people do when there's nothing much to hurry about. He showed us his cows and horses, and told us that firefighters were trying to put out a 5-acre forest fire caused by a lightning strike. He loaned Dad some fishing flies and told him about the secret fishin' hole by the windmill. We hurried back to the cabin so Dad could grab his gear and get there by sunset. Mom relaxed in her camping chair while Cheyenne and I happy danced around the edges of the pond until every fish was too afraid to eat anything.

We didn't get to eat fish for dinner that night, but Dad grilled some burgers and then played guitar until bedtime. There was a quiet peacefulness about that place, and none of us wanted to leave. We decided to come back in the fall when the aspen were changing.

The next morning Cheyenne and I played in the creek while Mom and Dad loaded up the truck. Then we stopped by to return the fishing flies Dad borrowed. The ranch hand looked worried and said the fire had grown to 50 acres and was only two miles away. He was getting ready to load up his horses and take them into town. Forest rangers were preparing to close down the main road to the ranch, and Kathy was calling all of the guests who were planning to rent cabins for the holiday weekend.

That fire blazed out of control for more than two months, destroying 24,000 acres of breathtaking forestland. The cabins were spared, but the fire prompted the owners to sell the ranch a few months later. We never got to return during the fall like we hoped, but we were very thankful that we had the chance to make lifelong memories in that wonderful place.

31

Posh Poodles and Unselfish Cats

One day my parents noticed that I was limping so they took me to see Dr. Guerrera, who happens to be one of the kindest people on the planet. I love him because he speaks softly to me and squats down to my level. He took x-rays of my front leg and then used some very big words to explain to my parents what was wrong with me. It sounded expensive to fix, and I could see my dad's face twitch a little bit. I tried to be on my best behavior for the next few days so he would decide I was worth repairing.

On the way back to the car, I noticed two poodles walking into the doggy day camp next door. I have never stayed there myself, but word has it that dogs can listen to classical music during naptime. Some owners pay extra so their pooch can sleep on a cot and watch television. I wondered what my rugged dog cousin, Pepper, would think about all that.

I knew money would be tight for the next few months because of my medical bills, so I took the initiative to enter myself in a pet photo contest, hoping to win free dog food for a year. Mom and I searched through my photos and submitted the maximum number of entries allowed. We chose pictures of myself with Froggy, baby Cheyenne, and foster puppies. I insisted on including one of me wearing my hiking pack. We had high hopes that we would win, partly because I'm so cute and also because hardly anyone else entered the contest. In the end I lost to a Husky snuggling up to a cat. It was very disappointing.

I was referred to a surgeon in a nearby town. In the waiting room I met a German Shepherd with an inverted testicle. I was embarrassed for him because his owner wasn't showing any discretion whatsoever. I'm pretty sure that if *I* had an inverted testicle (which I do not—because I'm a girl), my dad wouldn't just go around telling strangers.

A nurse took my parents and me to an exam room, and I was having a terrific time until I saw how many awards were hanging on the wall. I was worried Dr. Rooney would be a little bit stuck up, but Mom focused on the fact that he was very qualified and experienced. I worried for nothing. He walked into the room and plopped down on the floor next to me. He smiled a lot and gave me treats.

I needed surgery on both of my elbows to remove bone fragments. I was shocked, mostly because I had no idea that I had elbows. I thought they were knees. All this time people had referred to me as a "four-legged" creature, but I actually had two legs and two arms.

A nurse walked into the room with a piece of paper showing how much it would cost to make me all better. Dad threw up in his mouth a little bit. He asked what would happen if I didn't have surgery and she said I would be on pain medication and have arthritis for the rest of my life. I was only three years old, so I wasn't ready for assisted living. They drew my blood and scheduled my surgery. Luckily my parents signed up for pet insurance when they first adopted me because they figured it was a great way to prevent a divorce. Since they didn't have to pay for the whole surgery, they got to stay in love.

The nurse gave us a tour of the facility before we left. First she took us to see a secretary working in a little office. Behind her was an adorable Pug puppy resting in a tiny doggy bed. He had a cast on his leg—no wait, it was on his arm—and he looked a bit groggy. The nurse said he was recovering from surgery, and she thought he'd feel better if he wasn't left all alone.

Next we met a chubby cat named Fred who lived there on a permanent basis so he could donate blood whenever it was needed; he had already saved the lives of three other cats. We walked down the hall and saw a room where a dog was getting chemotherapy. That made Mom sad and she tried not to look. Then we turned the corner and a big dog in a kennel started barking at me as if I had wronged him in a past life. I decided to cut him some slack since he was probably having a rough day.

Two nurses asked if we could move along quickly because they were trying to draw blood from a black cat who was getting stressed out from the big barking dog. We hurried to an exam room where they had just taken care of a Schnauzer who had been bitten by a rattlesnake. Mom felt a little queasy just hearing about it.

Next we saw the room where my surgery would take place. There was a bright light above a metal table. Close to that was something that looked like a big TV screen to help Dr. Rooney do a really good job. Our tour guide showed us a secret passageway where a medical assistant could pass sterile instruments through the wall during surgery. I was very impressed.

On our way out, the nurse showed us a water tank where I would swim during my rehabilitation. My dad rolled his eyes when she said that, but I don't think she saw him do it. I agreed with my dad completely. I'm just a dog, for Pete's sake. Also I hate to swim. It's too risky.

32

Staples and the Blue Cone Monster

The morning of the surgery, my parents drove me to the vet and left me with a vet tech who had three bunnies that lived indoors. That's pretty much all I remember.

I woke up a few hours later and was shocked at my condition. My arms were completely shaven and there were staples (STAPLES!) in my elbows. Had someone confused me for a stack of papers?! I was outraged and ready to confront everyone who had violated me during my sleep… until I realized TO MY HORROR that someone had tied a terrifying Blue Cone Monster around my neck.

I knew my perpetrators wouldn't take me seriously if I approached them looking like that, so I decided to wait until my parents picked me up. I knew I could count on them to chastise the entire medical staff and demand that the cone—and staples— be removed immediately.

I had to wear the Blue Cone Monster for two whole weeks. Dad thought it made me look cute, as if I were playing the role of a blue flower in a school play. Cheyenne avoided eye contact with me and escaped to a far away room in the house, where she promptly threw up.

Dad gently carried me to the puppy pen that Mom had lined with soft pillows. I stood there and whimpered because I thought I deserved a lot of sympathy and extra attention. Dad made cheeseburgers for dinner while Mom sat in the pen and comforted me. She stayed with me all through the night so I wouldn't be sad and alone.

I spent the next day looking out the front window of the living room. Mom knew how much I liked to look out that window, so she had set up my pen right next to it. At first it was fairly exciting because I got to see some kids riding bikes and a large pit bull wearing a hot pink sweater. But then nothing happened for several hours and I started to lose the will to live.

Mom made an emergency trip to the library to borrow ten DVD's for me to watch while I recovered. One was called *Pony Play Date*. She thought I might like it—even though I'm terrified of horses—because there was a picture of a pig and a goat on the cover. She was wrong.

Mom made another poor choice by putting in the DVD *When Animals Attack*. Cheyenne flew off the couch and barked ferociously at the grizzly bear on the screen. I was startled and confused because I was doped up on painkillers. Mom quickly pressed Eject, and Cheyenne retreated back to the couch.

The next movie she tried was *Paw Prints of Thieves*. The main character was a Jack Russell Terrier dressed as Robin Hood. Mom liked the movie, but Cheyenne and I thought it was so boring that we fell asleep immediately.

Just when I started to lose hope that we would ever find a film we could all agree on, she popped in a National Geographic 3-DVD series called *Dogtown: Friends in Need*. Mom and Cheyenne joined me in my pen and we were all glued to the show. The actors used the words Sit and Stay to train dogs, so the plot was easy for Cheyenne and me to understand.

We saw a lot of homeless dogs with sad stories, but in the end most of them found nice families to love them. A little Shih

Tzu named Barney was rescued from a puppy mill. He had an eye infection, and his feet were full of sores from standing in his own poop. The vet fixed him all up and he got adopted by a nice lady in New York. A Dachshund named Parker was rescued from a puppy mill too. All of his teeth were rotten, so they had to be removed before the infection spread to his organs. Mom hates puppy mills, and that's why she tells her friends not to buy animals from pet stores (unless they are hosting an adoption event for a rescue group).

By the time the movie was over, I was no longer feeling sorry for myself. My fur would grow back and my staples would come out eventually. My limp would go away and I wouldn't have to wear the Blue Cone Monster forever. I had a family who loved me, and I couldn't ask for anything more.

33

High Fives and Wildfire Panic

My first physical therapy appointment was very exciting because I had not been allowed to leave the house for several days. I was so hyper in the waiting room that Mom worried I'd get hurt. A nice man came over and took us to a smaller room so I could get control of myself. He gave Mom some paperwork to fill out, and then the therapist came in and sat down on the floor in front of me. I liked her immediately.

She had some trouble coaxing me to stretch my paw up high near my ear, so Mom and Dad both said in unison, "Just say High Five!" So she did, and I cheerfully complied. Everybody laughed because I am so darn funny and cute. And smart. The doctor gave my parents a Take Home Exercise Program, which included five High Fives per paw each day. On my way out, I stood on my hind legs and begged for treats at the counter.

I was still wearing the Blue Cone Monster when I woke up one morning and smelled smoke in the house. Mom panicked and ran outside to see if there was a fire nearby. She couldn't see one, so she turned on the news. Sure enough, a forest fire was blazing out of control about an hour north of us. The wind was pushing the smoke our direction, but we weren't in danger.

That summer, Colorado set a new record for the most consecutive days over 100 degrees. Another huge wildfire flared up about one hour south of us. Hundreds of firefighters worked day and night to keep it from spreading to people's homes, but strong winds caused the fire to race down a mountain and 32,000 people were told to evacuate immediately. Everybody scrambled to grab what they needed and leave town before dark. Some folks were at work and couldn't get to their pets.

National news showed people walking their horses down the streets, and the President of the United States came to see the disaster with his own eyes. Everybody was glued to their televisions, and news coverage continued all through the night. When morning came, everyone was sad to see three hundred homes burned to the ground. The fire chief said he had never seen a fire behave like that before. Mom felt bad for the firefighters, the evacuees, and the animals. Cheyenne and I weren't that concerned because we were downstairs watching Dogtown for the third time.

My mom was lying on the couch beside my pen when she woke up and smelled smoke again. She turned on the news and sure enough, lightning had sparked another wildfire. This one was on the west side of us, and it was much closer: only ten miles away. Mom immediately put into action her life motto: You Never Need A Reason To Panic. She ran to her emergency stash and found her typed list of Things To Grab During An Emergency When You Aren't Thinking Clearly. She started a staging area in the living room, where she placed her suitcase and packet of important documents. She charged her cell phone, got a full tank of gas, and updated her collection of Insurance Pictures Of Everything We Own. She called Dad at work, and he made fun of her but then asked her to grab a few things for him.

Neighbors watched Mom load photo albums and dog food into the truck. They rolled their eyes and said there was no way the fire could travel all the way to our neighborhood. But she wasn't taking any chances. She had just seen the fire down south spread faster and farther than anyone thought possible. Fifteen wildfires surrounded us in Colorado that day. Most of them were blazing out of control, and Mom feared there weren't enough firefighters or fire bombers to put them out. She kept the TV on all night and slept with her tennis shoes on. We were ready to evacuate at a moment's notice.

We barely survived. Actually we didn't even have to evacuate. The fire stayed ten miles away from us, and a few days later Mom quietly took the photo albums out of the truck. She was proud of herself for overreacting and figured it was better to be laughed at for being over-prepared than to burn up in a heap of flames.

34

Strip Poker and Near Death

Eventually I decided that if the Blue Cone Monster wanted to kill me, it would have done so already. So I let my guard down and started sleeping at night instead of standing up and whimpering until I fell over from exhaustion.

My parents decided that since I was stuck indoors, it was a good time to do some home improvement projects so we could all be together. The tiny master bathroom needed some new flooring, and they figured it would only cost thirty bucks to put in some stick-on vinyl squares. But they were wrong because they forgot about the three rules of home improvement projects.

Rule #1: If you change one thing in a room, then you must change everything else in the room to match. My parents decided they might as well replace the crummy countertop at the same time they replaced the floor. And since countertops are usually sold with sinks attached, they figured they might as well get a new sink too. Heck, why not replace the vanity too so Mom could have a drawer for her toothbrush? In the end, my parents replaced not just the floor, but the countertop, sink, faucet, vanity, medicine cabinet, baseboards, toilet paper holder, outlet covers, caulk, and door hinges.

Rule #2: Your project will end up costing hundreds of dollars more than your original estimate. This is not just because you have to change everything to match, but also because you will break things you never planned to replace. In addition, you will find out that you don't own the tools required to complete the job correctly. This is why my dad had to replace the water valves under the sink and buy a fancy tool for trimming doorframes.

Rule #3: Your project will end up taking longer than you planned. The average home improvement project lasts longer than most marriages. This is not only because you will run out of vinyl floor tiles at midnight, but also because it's your spouse's fault for trimming the last square too crooked to fit right. Tension can be diffused by a spontaneous game of strip poker, but most divorce lawyers won't tell you that.

Two weeks after my surgery, I went to get my staples removed. Mom rolled the car windows down, and that caused the Blue Cone Monster to beat against my face. I didn't care because I was thrilled just to be out of the house.

Dr. Rooney kissed my forehead while he felt my elbows to make sure they were healing correctly. I passed the test and just like that, I didn't have to wear that dreaded blue thing around my neck anymore! I don't even have words to explain how glorious I felt at that moment.

Hydrotherapy was terrifying and exhilarating, like a roller coaster you don't want to ride but afterward you're glad you did. My physical therapist put a life jacket on me and gently hoisted me into the water tank. She smiled and Mom took pictures while I frantically tried to climb over the sides. Dad attempted to calm me down by holding a toy in front of me. I was dying and no one was making any effort whatsoever to rescue me.

A couple of minutes later I realized to my surprise that I was still alive and would probably live to see another day. I relaxed and swam my little heart out so everyone would be proud of me. When my therapist lifted me out of the tank, I had a big smile on my face and couldn't wait to do it again. But I never did get that chance because hydrotherapy is expensive and my parents are cheapskates.

35

Bristle and the Golden Blob

I had to take it easy for eight more weeks after I got my staples removed, so I passed the time by watching The Olympics from my pen. It was very boring until the announcer started talking about The Flying Squirrel. I had never heard of a squirrel that could fly. I closed my eyes and imagined the sheer joy that would surely come with leaping through the air in pursuit of a squirrel with wings!

I'm sure you can imagine my disappointment when I found out The Flying Squirrel was just a nickname for a girl who could launch herself really high into the air on something called The Vault. She was the very best gymnast in the whole wide world, and the announcers said she would win the gold medal for sure. They were wrong, and she was very disappointed in herself. I, however, was very impressed because she was ranked so much higher than everyone else that she was able to land on her butt—ON HER BUTT—and still win the silver medal!

I could never do anything like that, especially since I had put on a few extra pounds since my surgery. My nickname changed from the Golden Blur to the Golden Blob. Dr. Rooney said I needed to lose three pounds by going on a diet and slowly increasing the distance of my daily walks.

It seemed like a regular morning just like all of the other mornings. Mom took Cheyenne and me for a walk and nothing seemed unusual. Meanwhile at the elementary school just a few blocks away, a 10-year-old girl named Jessica had not shown up for her fifth grade class.

When Dad came home from work a few hours later, policemen were at the entrance to our neighborhood. They looked in his car and handed him a flyer with a picture of the pretty little girl. He saw hundreds of people walking side by side through a field. Volunteers searched the dog park (*my* dog park!) for signs of her. Divers investigated nearby ponds, and policemen knocked on door after door. Search dogs sniffed all over the area, trying their best to pick up her scent. The sky was filled with the sound of helicopters for several days, and we were very worried.

Jessica's parents posted a video of her on the Internet to help everybody recognize her. She had filmed herself with her little black and white dog, Bristle—just three days before she disappeared. I thought about that doggy and felt bad for her. I could tell she loved Jessica and wanted her to come back home.

Volunteers hung MISSING GIRL flyers everywhere. On mailboxes. Telephone poles. At the bank. In restaurants. Most of them had never met little Jessica, but they loved her anyway and wanted to do whatever they could to bring her home safely to her family. People tied hundreds of purple ribbons all over the city because that was Jessica's favorite color.

Some of Jessica's friends went to the park where she was supposed to meet a buddy on her way to school the day she went missing. They gathered some fall leaves and shaped them into a message that said "JESSICA COME HOME." People from all over town brought flowers and stuffed animals to that special place. Mom took me there and we left a purple bunny. I sat quietly and didn't even look for squirrels. Mom knelt down to read notes written by children who said they loved Jessica and wanted her to come home safely. It rained on our way home.

An hour later the police said they found her body in a field. It was the worst of news, but Mom felt comfort knowing that Jessica didn't have to be afraid anymore. She would feel no more pain. I felt sad for Jessica, her mom and dad, her friends, and her dog.

36

Fortune Cookies and Pessimists

My mom once opened a Chinese fortune cookie that read, "Hope for the best and prepare for the worst." She memorized it and put the little paper in her photo album. A few years later when she received an invitation to a Canine First Aid and CPR class, she was thrilled at the chance to finally apply the advice of the wise oriental snack.

Mom signed up for the course because she loves Cheyenne, foster puppies, and me. Dad signed up because he loves Mom (that's how he earned the Best Husband Award that year). The class was held at an upscale doggy daycare, so my parents got to see several wealthy dogs playing in the outdoor pool. They were wearing bright colored life vests that made them look very sophisticated and, of course, safe.

Quite a few people had eagerly gathered to take the CPR class. Odie, the instructor, was a funny guy who had been a human paramedic for many years. He asked everyone to introduce themselves and say why they were there. One lady said she was pursuing a career in dog massage and acupuncture. Another woman said she was starting up her own doggy daycare business. Mom said she wanted to be prepared in case Cheyenne or I got hurt at the dog park or in the mountains. Dad tried to look invisible.

Odie talked about the importance of owning a first aid kit. He pulled out each item and explained how to use it. He strongly advised everyone to buy a dog thermometer and immediately label it "DOG" so they didn't accidentally stick it in their mouth after it had been in their dog's... well, you know.

Next it was time for everybody to kneel down on the floor beside the canine mannequins. Dad raised his hand when the instructor asked if there were any optimists in the group, so Odie said, "This is for you." He played the song *Stayin' Alive* while my dad reluctantly blew into the plastic canine's mouth. Mom whispered, "I have never loved you more than I do at this moment."

Odie asked if there were any pessimists in the room and was surprised when nearly everyone raised their hands. Mom smiled and reasoned, "Why do you think we're here? It's because we're sure something bad is going to happen and we need to know what to do when it does!" Odie grinned and played a song for the worrywarts: *Another One Bites The Dust.*

My parents learned a lot during that class, and I felt better just knowing that they would know what to do if I ever showed symptoms of bloat, choking, heat stroke, snakebites, poison, bleeding, injured paw pads or broken limbs.

Mom splurged and paid an extra five bucks so she could attend the class for free as many times as she wanted (because she is very forgetful). She beefed up our doggy first aid kit and started carrying it with her whenever we went on walks. I'm sure the neighbors thought she looked dumb walking around the dog park with a little backpack, but it gave her peace of mind, and you can't beat that.

37

Boobs and Cinnamon Rolls

Word on the street has it that the best way for a woman to prepare for her first mammogram is to wedge her breast under the rear tire of a car and ask a stranger to back over it.

Thankfully I don't have to get mammograms even though I have several teats. My mom, on the other hand, has to get her chest smashed every year. She doesn't mind at all. In fact, she looks forward to it because the doctor's office has the relaxing aura of a luxurious spa. The lights are dim, the interior colors are beautiful, and the wooden doors have pretty frosted glass. She feels like a princess when the staff offers her a hot beverage and a heated robe. If they provided cinnamon rolls, she would get a mammogram every day.

Mom was sitting near the television in the waiting room when she heard the horrible news that a man had just walked into a school and taken the lives of some innocent kindergarteners. It was just a few days before Christmas. Mom had tears in her eyes when the nurse called her name.

Later that afternoon, Mom went to pick up some puppies to foster because animals are good to have around when you're feeling sad. When she arrived at the Nice Lady's house, everybody started whispering and smiling. They had a surprise... a whole litter of Husky mix puppies! When Mom saw them, her pupils swelled to the size of quarters, and her pulse sped up the way Dad's does when he walks into an electronics store. The 8-week old babies howled in their sweet little voices from the backseat on the drive home. Mom didn't stop smiling for three days.

The runt of the litter was only about four pounds, and he reminded my mom of Cheyenne when she was a tiny puppy. She named him Chester, and they were inseparable. When all of his siblings were busy wrestling, he climbed onto Mom's lap and sighed with contentment. She gave him a bath and then snuggled with him on the couch by Christmas tree light until he stopped shivering. She tried to stay up all night so she wouldn't miss one moment of gazing into his sweet soft face, but eventually she fell asleep.

She tied little reindeer antlers to his head the next morning, and took twelve million pictures of him. Mom was worried she might accidentally adopt Chester while Dad was at work, but the Nice Lady was ready to stage an intervention if necessary.

Having fostered almost 200 puppies, it's usually pretty easy for Mom to quickly drop her puppies off at Adoption Day and get on with her day. That was not the case with precious little Chester. She held him close and snuggled nose to nose while the pet store bustled with a huge crowd of people anxiously waiting to add a furry new member to their home. Eventually one of the puppy rescue volunteers gently pried Chester out of Mom's grip while she held back tears. He was the number one draft pick that day, adopted within two minutes by the first family who met him.

Cheyenne and I love to help Mom foster puppies, but we're always relieved when she drops them off so we can have her all to ourselves. Mom took turns petting us after she dropped off Chester, and then we got to go for a walk even though it was pretty cold outside. She told us about the kindergarten children and that got me thinking about Jessica, the little girl who was stolen from our neighborhood. Her family would be spending their first Christmas without her, and that made my heart hurt.

Mom and I agreed that we should do something to let them know we were thinking of them.

We went to the pet store so I could pick out a toy for Jessica's little dog, Bristle. There were so many toys to choose from that I had trouble deciding. Would she like something that squeaked? Should I get something that was good for chewing or soft for snuggling? Did she like to chase a ball or play tug-o-war? I put one thing in the cart and then took it back out when I saw something I thought she might like better. Just when I felt totally overwhelmed with such an important decision, I saw exactly what she needed: a purple stocking full of purple toys. A teddy bear, a football, a chew toy, and a tug-o-war rope.

We took the treasure home and attached a Winnie the Pooh bow. Mom wrote "To Bristle, With Love From Chipper" on the gift tag, and then we headed to the little park that had since been named after Jessica. The trees were still decorated with countless purple ribbons and pink butterfly wings just like the ones I had worn to the mall to support my friends in pediatric hospice. It was a beautiful sight to see, and we stood there quietly taking it all in. The stuffed animals we had seen months earlier were gone, but in their place were candles, flowers and poems written by Jessica's friends. We placed the purple stocking on the ground, and hoped our small gift would make Jessica's family feel loved.

38

Seagulls and New Beds

Mom and I decided to make our Christmas ornament fundraiser an annual tradition. Friends stopped by to help paint pink teddy bears and purple choo choo trains. Mom painted a bunch of cream-colored angels one night while she watched a sappy movie on television. She spread out the ornaments on the coffee table and Dad said it looked like she was decorating sugar cookies. The next day, he called her to the living room and asked if she knew what was all over the couch. Yes. Paint. Oops. It looked like a flock of seagulls had dive-bombed our sofa.

Friends and family bought enough ornaments to sponsor a very sweet little girl in a safe home for one year. Mom took great comfort in knowing that no bad men could hurt her. I wondered how many ornaments we'd have to sell for every child to be safe.

Cheyenne and I received more Christmas gifts than my parents did. They arrived in the mail, wrapped in colorful paper and smelling delicious (like peanut butter). The gift tags were signed by Santa himself. Grandma sent some money for Cheyenne and me to buy whatever we wanted. I stayed awake most of the night trying to decide which toy would best complete my collection.

The next morning, Mom told me that my Christmas money would be spent on a new dog bed because mine was getting smelly and lumpy. I'm sure you can imagine my disappointment. We went to four different stores before we found the right one (the one on sale). The cashier told Mom that her dog had THREE beds—one in the living room, one in the family room, and one in the bedroom! At first I couldn't figure out why her dog would need three beds unless he had narcolepsy. But then it struck me that perhaps he wasn't allowed on the couch. My mom would never buy me three dog beds even if she were a millionaire, because she is a tightwad.

When we got home, Mom put my new bed in the master bedroom and I tried it out. First I walked around in circles to get it good and fluffed, and then I plopped down. The new bed was significantly bigger than my last one, which meant I didn't have to curl up into a tight ball to fit my whole self onto it. I could stretch out completely and still have all of my parts surrounded by soft luxury. When I wanted to stretch out on my *old* bed, my nose and tail would touch directly against the carpet. I realized now how unacceptable that had been. My new gigantic bed smelled fantastic, so I decided to take a spontaneous nap and dream of squirrels.

Conclusion

Have you ever dreamed about something your whole life and then, once you achieved your goal, it turned out to be kind of a letdown? Well, that's how it was for me one chilly fall morning in the backyard. Cheyenne and I were just hanging out like we always do—providing free home security while my parents slept in—and that's when it happened. A fat brown squirrel suddenly appeared at the top of our fence, probably in search of nuts for winter.   Cheyenne remained motionless while I stealthily positioned myself against the fence. I had practiced for this day my entire life. I had a good feeling. This squirrel would be The One.

Mom awoke to the sound of me shrieking with excitement. Cheyenne immediately ran inside to tattle on me. Mom peeked out the window, saw me hovering over the lifeless creature, and ran downstairs to shut the doggy door before I could show her my amazing prize.   While she locked herself in the bedroom trying not to throw up, Dad quickly got dressed and headed to the back yard with a big plastic bag and some work gloves. Relieved that my furry conquest was still intact and not suffering, he made me Leave It while he scooped it up and threw it in the garbage. Then Mom brushed my teeth.

I'd had a lot of expectations for the day I caught my first squirrel. I had figured the city would throw a parade in my honor, probably at the dog park. I pictured my Dad carrying me through the crowd, hoisted atop his shoulders. Mom would pass around a petition declaring it a national holiday. Cheyenne, overcome with pride over her big sister, would skip through the crowd giving High Fives to people and dogs alike. News reporters would fight over themselves to interview me. Companies from all over the country would beg me to appear in commercials to promote their pet products. Magazines would feature full-length articles detailing my unique genetic blend of speed, coordination, and gracefulness.

None of those things happened, as hard as that is to believe. Instead we gathered around the garbage can in silence and held an informal funeral service. Mom gently suggested that I pay my respects by taking some time to think about my actions. So I took my medium-size self upstairs to my extra large bed because that's where I do my best thinking. I lay there with eyes open for a while, thinking about the world and my role in it.

I came up with a profound life lesson: *The Real Ones Don't Squeak.* I had assumed incorrectly that if I ever caught a real live squirrel, it would provide weeks of family entertainment, complete with exciting sound effects like my Squeaker the Squirrel toy. Nobody warned me that real squirrels aren't as much fun to play with after you catch them. They just lay there motionless, providing hours of disappointment and shame. It's true what they say. The thrill is in the wanting.

Eventually I figured out why my mom was disappointed in me: my purpose was to love, and what I did to that squirrel was not very loving.

A close friend once told my mom that she would appear smarter if she stopped talking. He was right. I once heard that most humans only use 10% of their brain. I don't know what the statistics are for the brain usage of dogs.

Personally I don't think it really matters how much of our brains we use. I think what matters is how much of our hearts we use.

There's a quote that says, "People don't care how much you know until they know how much you care." It's true. Mom loves Dad because he makes her feel special, not because he can quote any line from *Dumb and Dumber*.

I am not perfect. My front tooth is missing. I have an occasional limp. I don't get along with every dog I meet, and sometimes I bark at people for no reason. I thought I had to be a certified therapy dog in order to fulfill my destiny, but I was wrong. I don't have to be perfect to carry out my purpose of loving others. Maybe I will be a therapy dog again someday, but for now I'm having fun sharing my story with you. Wouldn't it be something if I ended up making more of a difference by being an author than a therapy dog? I guess it's true what they say. When one doggy door closes, another one opens.

Maybe somebody will read my book and decide to take a shelter dog for a walk. Or visit a nursing home. Or hug a veteran. What if—and this is just crazy talk—someone felt *so* inspired that they decided to take that shelter dog for a walk, then adopt him, get him certified as a therapy dog, and take him to a nursing home where he could hug a veteran?

Someone out there is waiting for a friend like you. Go out there and find them, even if you are a therapy dog dropout with a missing tooth and bad elbows.

Chipper's List:
25 Ways To Make A Difference

- Spay or neuter your pet
- Foster or adopt a homeless animal (Petfinder.com)
- Sponsor a child in an orphanage (PlantingPeace.org)
- Get involved in the fight against child sex trafficking (Love146.org, iEmpathize.org, Somaly.org)
- Offer encouragement to someone who is a caregiver for an elderly or disabled family member
- Mow the lawn for your friend whose spouse is in the military
- Serve a meal at a homeless shelter or children's hospital
- Foster or adopt a child
- "Adopt" a grandparent at a nursing home
- Join (or start) a Random Acts of Kindness group (Meetup.com)
- Turn your friendly, well-trained pet into a therapy animal
- Deliver valentines to sick kids at the children's hospital
- Donate warm coats to homeless people
- Mentor an at-risk youth
- Shovel snow or rake leaves for your elderly neighbor
- Volunteer for your local animal shelter or rescue group
- Do something nice for the single mom next door
- Volunteer to rock newborns at a hospital or orphanage
- Provide rides for people in need of kidney dialysis
- Encourage a victim of domestic abuse
- Sponsor a pizza party for homeless teens
- Deliver thank you notes to a group of veterans
- Participate in an activity at a disabled group home
- Sew a blanket or donate diapers to needy families with a newborn
- Decorate a cancer center for the holidays

I will donate 100% of the net proceeds from my gift shop to help rescue children and animals. I have a lot of fun merchandise such as greeting cards and ornaments featuring my foster puppy friends. You can also get T-shirts and jewelry with the logos below for yourself, your children, grandchildren, and pets to wear so others will know you belong to my circle of friends who brighten the world!

If my story inspired you to do something nice for somebody, I want to know! I would also love for you to send photos of your family, friends, and pets wearing your "Chipper's Friend" T-shirts! (If you send me a photo or story, you are giving me permission to use it in my scrapbook and on my Facebook page unless you say otherwise.)

ChippersFriends@gmail.com

For pictures, videos, and updates about me (and my foster puppy friends!), follow me on Facebook!

Facebook.com/ChippersFriends

If you liked my book, please leave a positive review on the site where you bought it, and recommend it to everyone you have ever met in your entire life.

Thank you!
Chipper

Acknowledgements
(from Chipper)

I would like to thank Kim, Brook—and all of the dedicated volunteers with the Colorado Puppy Rescue—for saving my life.

I would like to thank Bristle Ridgeway for letting me share the story of your precious Jessica. You are in my heart always.

I would like to thank my mom for loving me even though I'm not perfect.

I would like to thank my dad for letting me sit on the couch.

I would like to thank Cheyenne for showing me how to have a more comfortable Squirrel Surveillance experience by resting my elbows on the back of the couch.

I would like to thank Grandma for my Squeaker the Squirrel toy.